# I THOUGHT YOU'D NEVER ASK!

SIXTY-ONE OBSERVATIONS, COMMENTARIES, AND MUSINGS.

*by Upper Michigan Columnist*
*Frank R. Bartol*

*Enjoy!*

*Frank R. Bartol*

*with Illustrations by*
*Sheboygan, Wisconsin, Artist*
*Marie R. Hetzel*

Printed in Marquette, Michigan by Pride Printing, Inc. •⬭ 692-C

ISBN #0-9661412-0-2

*To Judith, who wasn't wild about my attempting another book but who stepped aside to cheer me on and stepped forward to offer her help whenever I needed it.*

# Contents

# CONTENTS

Green, white, and yellow are the basic colors of the spring season, but many maple leaves, in their budding stage, are red. For me the hills just outside of Munising offer one of the better spots to watch their metamorphosis into the lush green that will characterize U.P. woodlands come June. Again, one must be on the lookout for this beauty. It will not jump out at the passer-by, and when noted is more likely to elicit sighs of satisfaction than gasps of wonder and incredulity.

The nice thing about Nature's spring show is that there is no single right time to see it. Come to it a bit early and you'll not see many blossoms, but you can feast on the bronze and amber of the marshes, especially of the eastern U.P., and the special color of last year's grasses and weeds, which I can't come up with a term for. If you come to it late, you haven't necessarily missed the best part. It offers serial splendor right into June. Some of the late-season stars are marsh marigolds—-sometimes called cowslips—-in the swamps and dandelions in the meadows, which over-whelm the area with yellow. Blossoming sugar plum, cherry, and wild apple trees take over the job of adding whiteness just about the time the trillium blossoms begin to fade into the pale pinkness of their old age.

Unseasonably warm or unseasonably cold weather can affect the spring show schedule more than its autumnal counterpart, but your window of opportunity stays open a long time. Take advantage of that to observe a phenome-non which may now get the attention it deserves— if the name I've just given it sticks.

Someday the world of commerce may discover it, too, and dwellers in the asphalt and concrete world of our cities will start coming here in droves in April and May to fill our motels and other tourist facilities during this inappropri-ately named "off season," which is really as "on" as our awareness of it permits it to be.

# Books: My Mother Helped Me to Love Them

∽

There may be some special days during the course of the year that I would have a tough time using over and over again as subject matter for an essay. But Mother's Day is not one of them, because mothers enrich the lives of their children in such a diversity of ways that if I were to select one each year from the mother lode, I wouldn't exhaust it for decades.

I'm grateful that my mother is still around to read the message that follows. It is my Mother's Day card to her and to all the other mothers who will recognize themselves in it.

Perhaps I would have developed my love for language and literature in the absence of my mother's nurturing efforts in that direction, but I'm inclined to think not. The spark she detected in me as a little boy she blew into a flame, which she continued to fuel throughout my growing up years. My father was generally supportive of her efforts, but I don't think I'm being unfair to him in giving her the lion's share of the credit.

Books are part of my earliest memories. My mother saw to that by presenting me with one or more every Christmas. I grew up during the Great Depression, when gift giving, if it was possible at all, was limited to Christmas time in most families. If that had not been the case in our house, I'm sure she would have presented me with a book or two for my birthdays as well.

One of my early favorites was a thick book, with big print appropriate for my seven or eight years and many illustrations, in black and white, of bugs of various kinds engaging in some kind of warfare. To this day when I reminisce with other family members about some of those early books, we bring that one up and wonder why we have never located it in some box or other up in the attic, where so many of our childhood things are stored. Perhaps it's just as well, because that book probably wouldn't fare very well today under the kind of critical scrutiny our adult minds would bring to it.

I cut my reading teeth on the standard fare of the time, which included *Grimm's Fairy Tales* and other books of fable and fancy, and as I grew older I followed Tom Slade around to a lot of places, including Temple Camp.

When I started to record my age with double digits, I was presented with Zane Grey's *Riders of the Purple Sage* and just about every other book he had written. It was fairly easy for my mother then, because Zane's text was pure as the driven snow. My mother's zeal in protecting us kids from "indelicate material" makes Thomas Bowdler look like a rank amateur. And when she made a mistake in selecting a book whose title didn't warn her about the smutty (by her standards) road ahead, she very neatly excised all the pages containing offensive material.

One such book was *Uncle Tom's Children,* whose title suggested that it was a sequel to that famous nineteenth century novel and not the twentieth century one about the life of blacks, written by Richard Wright. Her scissors worked overtime on that one but enough of the book remained to give me an early-life feel for what things were like for blacks back then and helped shape me into as unbigoted a person as a kid growing up in the U.P., where there were virtually no blacks living in those days, could be.

Snobs may carp at the absence of literature with a capital "L" in the examples I've cited thus far. There was no *Pilgrim's Progress* or *Paradise Lost* in my boyhood reading, for which I'm eternally grateful, but the pleasant feel of less weighty books in my hands then led me to great works later, when I was ready for them——though I confess that I was never able to work my way through *Pilgrim's Progress.*

When I reached my late teens, my mother gave up on trying to select fictional reading material for me and turned to such titles as *Bartlett's Familiar Quotations, The Complete Works of Robert Frost,* and an occasional dictionary. She even presented me once with a book of Edgar Guest's works, that too-often maligned versifier, who admittedly wrote stuff that wasn't great poetry, to say the least, but gave me a feel for rhyme and rhythm which I used as a stepping stone to it later.

It was Guest who wrote that "it takes a heap o' living in a house to make it home," a pretty profound idea, however simply it was expressed by him. And I'm glad that "living" at our place included long winter evenings near a wood Heatrola stove with a good book in hand. Thanks, Mom.

# A Wedding to Remember

∾

We have now begun the month whose greatest claim to fame is that it is the one in which most marriages take place here in the United States. Surveys probably wouldn't support that claim any more, at least not if my relatives and friends are counted in them—Judith and I haven't been to many June weddings in recent years.

But we've just returned from a May one up in Grand Marais, Minnesota, that I started pronouncing a "darn-close-to-perfect" event almost from the moment we began the drive a third of the way around Lake Superior to get to it. Accustomed to being excited by that lake's beauty and grandeur as I watched it lap our Upper Michigan shoreline over the years, I had to admit that it did a pretty respectable job of lapping at Minnesota shores, too.

It was momentarily disconcerting to know that, once we arrived in Grand Marais, we had to go up Gun Flint Trail and turn left on Maple Hill Cemetery Road to get to the church, because neither of those names conjures up images appropriate to a wedding. But we found that little non-denominational chapel right where the map said it would be, and as soon as I laid eyes on it I knew that we were back in "darn close to perfect" territory again.

It was an unpretentious structure—a generic country church, it might be called, with its narrow beveled siding, painted white, and its bell-tower-over-vestibule design. Its interior, except for a small railed-off area in front, was filled with pews constructed of oak stained a rich brown. I counted those pews and determined that they would accommodate eighty people and that the empty spaces in them would just about hold the folks I estimated were still engaged in friendly conversation outside the chapel when we entered it. (I am an almost obsessive pew counter and crowd calculator at weddings).

I was intrigued by the building's windows, only two of which were made of stained glass. The other four afforded us a good view of the woods between us and Lake Superior, which I could almost see and whose presence I certainly felt. My gaze was then directed to a quilt hanging on the front wall. Each of its sixteen panels illustrated a significant event in the lives of the guests of honor, and it was obviously created by folks who had more than a modicum of artistic talent. It took only a few more moments for me to find out that artistic talent is not something in short supply in the little community of Grand Marais. Mesmerized by the rustic charm of the inside of the chapel, I didn't notice four musicians up front and to our left until I heard the first notes of beautiful music they would continue to produce before and throughout the ceremony.

A dulcimer, a flute, a hand-held drum (it probably has another name), a short wooden pipe, and a guitar were the instruments they wielded so professionally. But one of them had an additional instrument that outdid them all: her voice. A beautiful lady, she had the kind of stage presence that told me she could have handled Carnegie Hall with the same grace and charm she demonstrated in the little chapel at the end of Maple Hill Cemetery Road, just off Gun Flint Trail, in Grand Marais, Minnesota. And the quality of her voice announced that she would not have been out of place in that large concert hall.

When the bride walked down the short aisle to the front, in a simple but pretty gown she had made herself, the tableau was complete, and I had a moment to reflect on how timeless it was. This wedding could just as well have been happening in 1897, 1797, or even 1697. Our cars were out of view alongside the gravel road behind the church, so there was nothing of the modern world intruding upon us: no microphones, no speakers, and, though a lovely chandelier hung down from the center of the church, no artificial lighting, because Mother Nature was cooperating that day with plenty of sunshine, which had no trouble finding its way through those windows of unstained glass.

I have always said that there can be no good wedding without a minister, priest, or rabbi truly willing to participate in it instead of just mouthing words, and the minister there that day participated with exuberance, sincerity, and talent that held us in his thrall from the moment he first announced his presence from the back of the chapel by saying, in a strong but melodious voice: "Look at where we are!" It was not a particularly religious opening, but it was converted into one later, and it was uttered with such joy and fervor that it set the tone for all that followed.

We married people in attendance were remarried by him that day as he reminded us of our commitments to each other. And the young people there had to be saying: "If I ever take the plunge, he's the guy I want to have doing the honors for me."

Let the record show that I have also attended weddings

that have impressed me in churches twenty times the size of the chapel my cousin David was married in last Saturday and a hundred times as grand. But there was something about this particular wedding that will have me remembering it for a long time. And I think I know what it is: eighty people in a church that will hold eighty is a much more intimate environment than two hundred people in a church that will hold two thousand. And the voices of minister, singer, and two young people pledging their troth do not get lost in the confines of a room not much larger than most living rooms.

Given the urban nature of today's society, most of the Davids and Beckys who were married last Saturday across the United States could not have a ceremony in a tiny white church, way out in the country "far from the madding crowd," but I hope that they all found something to sustain and gladden them in what continues to be a momentous event wherever it occurs, and whether it takes place in May or December.

# Gardening: I'm Committed,
# Come What May

∾

I am writing this piece on May 12th, and today Mother Nature is making her fifth effort this month to dissuade me from putting in a garden this year. The temperature is hovering in the very low forties, and snow mixed with rain is being blown past my office window by a northwest wind.

But I know that by the time you read these words in a couple of weeks, I will be as deeply committed to that 50 x 150 foot plot of soil behind the big chicken coop on the home place as I ever was.

I went by that plot early last Saturday, and when I saw the corn stalks I hadn't had a chance to remove last fall and the long section of fencing that had been pulled away from the fence posts by the record-breaking snows of last winter, I said to myself: "This is an excellent time to become an ex-gardner."

But I made the mistake of continuing my walk past the only active farm left in Traunik. The smell of cow manure recently spread on a field right next to the road reminded me of a ritual with which I have begun the gardening season every year since taking over vegetable-raising responsibilities from my mother almost a decade ago.

I am well conditioned now to respond to the essence of cow dung on a spring day by hitching a trailer to my old 9N Ford tractor and heading for the manure pile behind the barn on Bill Debelak's now inactive dairy farm for some well-aged manure. Which is precisely what I did as soon as I returned from my walk, but not before I slipped on a pair of high rubber boots, and not until I had stopped in at the apartment Bill now occupies in Traunik for permission to fork on a load of the stuff he had forked out of his barn before retiring several years ago.

I really had no choice in the matter. That whiff of cow manure set off a chain of events that I had to engage in, no questions asked. Perhaps if Bill had said no to me this time, that would have broken the chain. But he didn't—never has—and the pile of manure, though now substantially smaller than it was a few years ago, looks as if it's good for at least a dozen more years—though I'm not sure I am.

And if my mother, just once, didn't say to me when spring arrived: "You ARE planning to have a garden this year, aren't you?" that, too, might break the chain. That's a break I don't look forward to, though I know it's coming, because at age ninety-one, mostly confined to her house after a hip fracture almost two years ago, she's not likely to be around for too many more years to ask it.

She did again, right on schedule this year. If she hangs on for just a while longer, by the time she stops asking the question, I'll be talking to myself even more often than I do now and, in deference to her memory, I'll do both the asking and affirmative answering myself.

The truth is that I garden as much for her as for myself. Until a couple of years ago, she often came up to the fence around my garden, looked in on me as I worked, and called my attention, gently but yet firmly, to my failures and mistakes, offering corrective advice as she did so. But she was also quick to praise my successes, however modest they might be compared to what she had been able to accomplish.

My mother was one of the best gardeners in our community. She always planted later than everyone else, and in early June she had to endure the bragging of some of her lady friends as they told her and each other about how high their beans were already, this at a time when my mother hadn't even planted hers.

But we were eating garden beans at our house ahead of just about everybody else, because she had the greenest of green thumbs. And it didn't hurt to have a garden located on ground that had been a chicken yard for a quarter of a century!

So yesterday morning, before the weather turned bad, I picked up all those dried corn stalks and roto-tilled that manure into the ground. Now, I can only look out my window for enough of a break in the weather so that I can at least stick onion sets into that freshly-turned earth and plant peas up against a chicken wire fence that they'll be climbing before the rest of the garden is in.

After that happens, I'll wait for a planting signal from my retired gardening consultant, and I'll spend some time daydreaming about those burgundy beans, purple on the vine but turning a vivid green in the cooking pot, which I enjoy so much cooked together with slender, young garden carrots over which I pour melted butter (in modest amounts, Dr. Bjork!). And I'll think about those first ears of sugar and cold corn and the tomatoes that usually ripen about the same time.

I'll also savor the prospect of bringing my successes into my mother's house for the pat on the head that I cherish as much at age sixty-seven as I did when I was a little boy—we are forever little boys in the presence of our mothers. My failures I'll leave in the garden that she can no longer visit: the kohlrabi turned woody, the cabbage half eaten by worms, etc.

I DON'T look forward to having to cover frost-sensitive plants (which is to say, almost all of them) against a late-spring assault by below-freezing temperatures. Nor will I be too happy when I spot the hoof prints of the deer that almost always manage to vault just an inch higher than the top wire on my garden fence. And I have no enthusiasm for the interminable weeding that awaits me, or the watering that will be required during a late summer drought.

But if you come through Traunik anytime after Memorial Day, there's a good chance you'll find me working my garden. That whiff of manure, my mother's almost-rhetorical question, and a deep-down sense that that's what Fate has decreed I should do with some of my retirement time will keep me at it until a planting occurs that I will be involved in but have no awareness of. That one I'm willing to postpone for a while!

# The Dreaded After-Dinner Yawner

ॐ

Last week I fell victim to the dreaded after-dinner yawner. I had heard about him a couple of times from people whose careers resulted in their frequent appearance as guest speakers. But the demand for such services from English teachers, retired or active, tends toward the minuscule. So I was spared the indignity of a closeup look at a dangling uvula until this past summer, when the publication of my first book of essays produced half a dozen invitations to be on one program or other.

These I accepted enthusiastically, partly because they almost always resulted in a book sale or two, and also because, after seven years away from the classroom, I still hanker to stand before a group of people and hold them in thrall with gems of wisdom never before uttered, interspersed with witty off-hand remarks, all delivered with perfect timing in a voice that helps fill the room with my presence.

Of course, hundreds of students have yawned at me over the years to tell me that my perception of what was going on as I spoke was different from theirs. But those yawners never bothered me, because in classrooms they gravitate toward the back of the room whenever possible, leaving the front desks for those apple polishers who have cultivated the ability to assume a look of rapt attention, which they hope will improve their chances for a good grade.

But adult yawners at dinner functions apparently don't head for the far corners of the room. These otherwise-decent folks, who have absolutely no intention of ruining a speaker's evening, generally accomplish that end nevertheless by placing themselves just opposite the speakers' lectern—usually within six feet of it.

My yawner was a big man, so ignoring him would not have been easy no matter where he had been seated. But there in front of me he represented a visual obstacle that I just couldn't get around. Not that I didn't try, for both his sake and mine, because I could see that he was making heroic efforts to stifle all twenty-five of those yawns (give or take one or two), and the apologetic expression on his face at the end of each one was almost as hard to take as the yawn itself.

The urge always seemed to come upon him at a point in my performance where I thought I was really on a roll. For example, I was reading a poignant passage from an essay on the death of my German shepherd, Duke, which I would have expected to wring tears from Attila the Hun. But I looked up immediately after what I thought was a powerful concluding sentence right into yawn number 14—one of the more impressive ones of the evening both in intensity and duration.

All in all, though, I had a good time there that evening, because wide-awake listeners were still in the majority. And I forgave the yawner because I've been one myself often enough over the years.

The physiological explanation for post-prandial sleepiness is that as soon as one's stomach is filled with food, increased blood supply is sent to the digestive area to get that job done, thus reducing the amount going to the brain. The yawn, I understand, is just an effort by the body to set things back in balance.

I wish, though, that program planners would schedule speeches before dinner. Granted, speakers would have to deal with the glares of hungry guests beginning to salivate in anticipation of food whose aroma is wafting in from the kitchen area, but that would be a situation easier to deal with than close-up yawners.

I have one residual concern: the gentleman I've been describing did not stop by after the program to buy one of my books, as several of the other guests did. So maybe it WAS my performance rather than his full stomach which triggered all those yawns—as unbelievable as that seems.

# The "Yooper" Dialect:
# As Good As Any Other!

∾

When I told someone in a downstate business place recently that I was from the Upper Peninsula, he looked surprised and said: "You could have fooled me; you don't talk like a Yooper." I could tell by the expression on his face that he thought he was paying me a high compliment. And I suspect that he knew immediately from the expression on mine that I didn't receive it as such.

I'm sure it's no secret to anyone who has read more than a few of my essays that I am a Yooper born and bred and will rise to the defense of our beautiful U.P. and its people whenever I hear it or them maligned or denigrated by an "outsider," even though I have been, and will continue to be, mildly—and sometimes even harshly—critical of certain aspects of my home turf. After the brief lesson that courtesy and good U.P. breeding permitted me to teach this individual, it was no secret to him either.

I offer that same lesson in a slightly expanded form here to anyone from downstate or out of state who may be inclined to think that we talk funny up here and to my fellow Yoopers who might at some time have felt self conscious or defensive when confronted with that observation.

The simple truth is that everyone talks funny to someone who is from a different geographical area. That funniness is called "dialect," and a good dialectologist can pinpoint, often within a hundred miles, where a person is from by listening to him talk and by asking him what he calls a particular object or activity. I call a certain edible something a pancake, someone else says it's a flapjack, and a third somebody refers to it as a griddlecake, and in so doing we all help the dialect expert identify where we're from.

I won't go into very much detail about those language differences which constitute an Upper Peninsula dialect (which, by the way, is not a totally accurate term, because there are detectable dialect differences WITHIN the U.P., too), but one that gets mentioned by almost all those who would ridicule our Yooper dialect merits some explanation—and defense—here. That term is "eh," which is most often used to express anticipated agreement with a statement: "That was a good movie, eh," for example.

Some linguistic experts say that "eh" was imported to our area from Canada. However it arrived, it now tends to be a Yooper identifier. The term itself simply reveals a felt need in many languages for some kind of affirmation or agreement particle. Germans sometimes say "nicht wahr" in that spot, the French, "n'est-ce pas," all three terms meaning: "is that not true?" One could argue that "eh" is the most efficient of the three in that it requires the uttering of only one syllable instead of two, but it has not established the reputation of the other two as a "legitimate" expression.

Quite a few dialect differences result from languages brought to an area by immigrants. Up here, Finns are a dominant ethnic group. The Finnish language emphasizes the first syllable of almost every word. That pattern carries over into English to produce DEtroit instead of DeTROIT, as does the absence of the "th" sound in Germanic and Slavic languages, which produces "dese" instead of "these." Our ethnic heritage is very close to the surface here, linguistically and otherwise.

Linguistic experts could explain the reasons for most dialectal differences, but that's not important to most of us. What is is acceptance of the idea that there is nothing intrinsically better or worse about one dialect than another, though admittedly some have developed a better social or business reputation and thus are imitated by those striving to "make" it in either of those areas.

A Yooper dialect in its more exaggerated form may very well close some doors of opportunity in the professional world, and one may want to adapt speech patterns to that reality. In doing so, though, be forewarned that you will be contributing to that same homogenization in language that has occurred in so many other aspects of American life, much to its overall detriment, I think.

So go out there and speak your particular form of the English language with a little more confidence and pride. And the next time someone makes a disparaging remark about it, just remember that it's his ignorance that's being revealed and not yours, eh.

# Elvis Stamp Nothing but a Hound Dog

∾

There are a lot of places where one might have found me on the day that the Elvis Presley commemorative stamp was issued, but in line at the post office to buy some of those stamps was not one of them.

I do not number myself among Elvis's fans, though I think he had a remarkable singing talent that tended to get lost among all those gyrations, rhinestone suits, and other things that became his hallmark. Countless times since his death I would listen to a song on my car radio, be impressed by the quality of the singing, and then learn that it had been recorded by none other than Elvis the Pelvis.

His talent is no longer in question in most musical circles, but his character always will be as far as I'm concerned. Practically elevating him to sainthood in the years since his death, with a coronation of sorts occurring with the issuing of a stamp in his honor, is just another sign that our society really is going to hell in a handbasket. No one has yet suggested that he filled his body with drugs to protect innocent young children from them, but in the deification process which continues apace that might well happen.

However, my main point has less to do with Elvis than with this whole business of selecting folks who have made some sort of impact upon society (more and more it doesn't seem to matter what kind) and honoring them with commemorative stamps. I really think the U.S. Postal Service's only business should be to deliver the mail, a job which it has been doing far better than it is currently fashionable to give it credit for.

When it gets involved with a project like the Elvis stamp, which practically everyone knows it is doing for one reason only—to make lots of money—then it is getting mired in the crass world of merchandising, where all too often just about anything goes. If Elvis can generate so much postal income now, won't Sinatra, or Madonna, or some other well-known entertainment figure be considered for some future campaign?

And how about the possibility of selling advertising space on stamps? I can just see the Big Three feverishly outbidding each other for the right to picture one of their new models on first-class stamps and paying extra for a "Buy one of ours" slogan printed on each envelope as it is being cancelled.

Even when a person being commemorated with a stamp is not offensive to a segment of society, his or her face may not be appropriate in a particular situation. Recently we were about to mail a sympathy card to a friend but were reluctant to affix to the envelope the only stamp we had in our possession at the moment, which featured a picture of a clown, or a comedian, or some such figure. Practicality and convenience won out in that instance, but I wish we would not have been confronted with the issue in the first place.

Frankly, I think the design, size, and color of the stamp required to mail a first class letter should be standardized, with only the number printed on it to indicate its cost changing from time to time. The first dollar bill I ever earned was green and had a picture of George Washington on one side. Today's dollar looks pretty much the same. I like that. And it is still the same size, so I don't have to change billfolds to accommodate it. There is so much variety in other aspects of our lives that a little boredom and predictability in postage stamps would not be such a bad idea.

I bought a stamp recently that was so long I had to lay it on its side on the envelope so it wouldn't hide the address. I wasn't comfortable doing that because I recall from my youth that putting a stamp on an envelope upside down was supposed to convey a message of love to the addressee. What laying one on its side might be taken to mean I have no idea, but to me it just didn't look right in that position.

I suspect that most of my philatelist friends stand ready now to point out that their interesting hobby could not exist if governments would take my advice. I know that as well as the next guy, but the United States Postal Service has enough problems dealing with things that are germane to its existence. I don't think it should be concerned about keeping a small segment of our population entertained.

But I'm pleased to note that it is now possible to buy stamps with a no-lick adhesive backing. I hope the stamp that triggered this piece is of that type. The last thing in the world I want to do when I mail a letter is lick the back of Elvis Presley's head!

# The Chicken Dance: I Hate It

❧

I don't know whether what I'm about to acknowledge represents a character flaw in me or not, but in the interest of representing myself as I truly am, I feel obliged to tell my readers that I hate the chicken dance. Given that that dance is apparently written into the contract of every single polka band of whatever ethnic persuasion these days and has infiltrated a number of wedding receptions, with a good many folks responding to it with enthusiasm, I think it brave of me to make this admission, and I'm willing to do so only under the protective cover of time and distance afforded me by this mode of communication.

Anyway, I watched some attractive and otherwise dignified middle-aged and elderly folks doing this dance on a locally produced television show just half an hour ago, and my hands, always somewhat cold except in mid-summer, became more so, and a chill ran up and down my spine as I remembered how hastily I had retreated to the sidelines when the band leader announced the chicken dance during last year's Fourth of July Slovenian polka dance at the Traunik Hall.

Without fail that dance gets plugged into the program just when I have fine-tuned my polka step to the point where I can imagine the non-dancers casting admiring and envious glances my way and calling the attention of their fellow watchers to the rhythmic and graceful way I am able to maneuver my partner past and around the less-gifted performers.

That evening I had really hit my stride and was prepared to polka the evening away, so I resented having to abandon the floor to people who were about to squat, strut, flap their wings, and run around in circles much the way those thousands of chickens did on the poultry farm where I had grown up (do I detect the furrowing of a psychiatric brow or two?).

Dancers, if one wants to be cynical—and truthful—about it, can look pretty silly even when they're not trying to, so the process of working oneself up psychologically and emotionally to a state where he sees the beauty that also exists in dancing is a delicate one which can ill afford the comic relief of the chicken dance.

The music to which that dance is done is basically that of the schottische, which is very pleasant played at the correct tempo. But that tempo is always increased at the end so that the "chickens" cannot possibly stay in rhythm, and some wind up squatting while others are flapping their wings or twirling around in circles. Some of the positions that are assumed, if duplicated by an actual chicken, would produce either an egg or something that the dancers would be likely to slip on.

At some point the dancers form a large circle, change partners, and do a few other things that are supposed to help people "mix." What always amazes me is that at the end of the dance, when squatting, strutting, wing flapping,

and other chicken-like activities produce a frenzy of anatomical extremities in motion, the participants seem to be having the time of their lives.

As for me, when that number is concluded (it is often followed by an intermission to allow the dancers time to catch their breath), I am totally unable to get in the mood to polka again. Having watched the back ends of several ladies with whom I had danced earlier writhe and twitch at about the same altitude at their heads—a sobering experience, I cannot regain the perception I had of them as sophisticated, graceful, attractive people.

The thought of asking someone who had just been a chicken to dance is more than I can deal with, so I spend the rest of the evening concentrating very hard on watching "normal" dances so that I'll have the courage to return to the next polka dance that appears on our social schedule.

Deep down, though, I'm a liberal fellow, and would not, if appointed cultural czar, outlaw the chicken dance— different strokes for different folks and all that. But I would insist it be the last one of the evening so that folks who feel the way I do could escape from the dance hall and head for home, where, if there were any chickens on the premises, they had long ago gone to roost.

# Father's Day: Do We Men Deserve One?

∞

L ike most fathers across the country, I enjoyed Father's Day. My younger son treated me to dinner, and I in turn treated my father. The three of us sat at a window table at one of my favorite out-of-the-way eating places in the area, the Camel Rider's Restaurant, enjoying the food, the magnificent scenery, and—most important—each other's company. Afterwards, we took the backroads home, across what we used to call the blueberry plains. Had Judith and my mother been with us, that would have been a no-no because neither of them has ever seen a gravel road that she liked. And both get panicky when there is the slightest uncertainty as to where that gravel road might lead.

So without the direct involvement of any women except those who served us at the restaurant, we celebrated the day that is set aside to honor fathers. The euphoria thus engendered could have lasted at least past Monday if I had not started the week, as I always do, by watching the early news on TV, switching later to the radio as I ate breakfast, and then, still later, reading two daily newspapers.

When I realized that men, a substantial proportion of whom are fathers, were making most of the news that one could call bad, it occurred to me that while it's okay for us fathers to feel good about that status, we should be more than a little concerned about the maleness which is its prerequisite.

The specific story which triggered this thought was yet another news article about a man shooting his estranged wife and then himself to death. These events are so commonplace now that news media may soon begin to report in detail only those which involve women as perpetrators on the theory that "man bites dog" is news while the reverse is not.

That's very sad. Why is is that women—at least most of them—can deal with the breakup of romantic relationships by picking themselves up, dusting themselves off, and then going on with their lives, while we men all too often grab a gun (the weapon of choice in a country where one is always within easy reach) and end it all?

Psychiatrists partially blame such behavior on hormones like testosterone, and sociologists talk about the historic role of the male as protector of the family etc. But that doesn't change the bottom line, which is that we men are a violent breed. What scares me most is that the veneer of civilization, which ought to be getting a bit thicker over the centuries, seems to be wearing away to the point where we are now no better than our most savage ancestors, and modern technology is geometrically multiplying our capacity to harm our human fellows.

When next you see a riot or some other violent event on the TV evening news, take a close look at who's turning over those automobiles, torching that building, throwing stones at the police, or looting those stores if you want some evidence to support my thesis. Or go down to your local police station to see who is being hauled in for one violent infraction of the law or other.

Let's face it, men: our track record is dismal—and not getting any better. Even when we turn our attention away from violent crimes, we fare much worse than women. We're simply more inclined to lie, cheat, and steal than our female counterparts—though some of them are getting better at those things in the present equal-rights-for-women environment.

As for our general behavior: watch us at baseball games swilling down beer, shouting obscenities at umpires, stripping to our waists in the hope that some TV camera will zoom in on our hairy chests, and doing other boorish things, while the male players on the field cover the ground with their spit.

I am a gentle person, who swears only when severely provoked (though I confess to being severely provoked more often than I ought to be), and I never spit. And, yes, I have known women who do both. And, yes, a lot of us men are nicer than our wives and daughters. But we're talking percentages here, guys, so let's not take refuge in those exceptions.

I grew up on a chicken farm, where there were five thousand hens and nary a rooster. The roosters which had gotten past the chicken sexers at the hatchery were early on plucked from the flock and sold for meat before they could begin to do their roosterly thing. Only a few were kept alive into adulthood back at that hatchery for breeding purposes.

What worries me is that women of the world will someday tire of our behavior and do the same with us. Just recently two well known female political figures were named to the highest office in their countries. If that portends a trend, in a couple of decades most world leaders could be women! Maybe we men ought to start thinking about getting our act together and try harder to prove that we deserve to hang around so that Father's Day can still be celebrated well into the twenty-first century.

# Spare Me Plastic Flowers on Graves

∾

From time to time in these essays I like to tell my readers what I would do "if I had a magic wand." Well, what I would do on Memorial Day is wave it to make every artificial flower on every grave in the country disappear.

I don't think I am either stupid or insensitive. If I were the former, it wouldn't occur to me that those flowers were probably put there by folks who will be hurt and offended by what I've already said and am about to say. If I were the latter, I wouldn't care.

Well, I do care. And I know very well that my position on this issue will lose me more friends than it will gain me, because, let's face it, the number of people who use artificial flowers to decorate the graves of their loved ones probably constitutes a majority.

But Henry David Thoreau devised another majority when he said: "Any man more right than his neighbor constitutes a majority of one." I am sure enough of being that special majority in this case to plunge onward with my argument, recognizing, of course, that rightness in this matter is a highly subjective thing.

I am not opposed to artificial flowers in any interior setting in which I've encountered them in recent years. I look every day at a vaseful on our mantel that I think decorates the place nicely. But I have never seen an artificial one, whether of silk or plastic, that looks truly in harmony with the great outdoors. And I have only rarely spotted one that makes a grave look nicer than the natural grass, or even weeds, that it was placed among.

For a few days it may pass muster, but in a short time, under the onslaught of rain and sunshine that its for-real counterparts thrive on, its color, never natural, begins to fade. Even if it doesn't, when that rose, lily, or carnation continues to "bloom" out of season, the kindest word I can use to describe it is "grotesque," especially when that blossom protrudes from November snows, which mercifully get deep enough by the end of that month up here to hide it from view for a while.

To me the main function of flowers on a grave is a symbolic one. They signify the continuation of life even in the presence of death. The person who plants them there is affirming his belief in the interconnectedness of us all, living and dead.

This past week, in preparation for the upcoming Memorial weekend, I put a pair of red geraniums on the grave of my best friend, those flowers chosen because they were his favorites in life. I'm well aware that they will probably get zapped by frost or, escaping that, fall victim to an overzealous sun and an accompanying drought later on. One or the other fate has befallen them four of the six years that I've planted them there. But twice I was able to visit my friend's grave in midsummer and see them blossoming in all their red glory. That felt good.

I also planted some marigolds on the graves of my

grandparents and other relatives in the Munising cemetery, saving a couple for the grave of one of my father's very good bachelor friends, the only flowers ever planted there, to the best of my knowledge. In performing that little ritual, I brought these folks back to life in my memory in a way that I never can in any other place at any other time.

During my visits to several cemeteries recently, I watched people spade up the ground, plant this year's flowers, and bring water to them to give them a start, and I could sense that they were making important connections with those who had gone before them. But I also saw a good many plastic floral arrangements that I remember being there last year, the year before that, and, judging from their decrepit appearance, probably for at least a decade.

I simply cannot buy the argument that natural flowers aren't "practical" here in the U.P., where we are assured of only three frost-free months each year. If practicality were a consideration, plastic flowers would have replaced real ones in everybody's yard. Sad to say, I'm beginning to see them there but in nowhere near the profusion that they can be found in cemeteries these days.

Plastic is a non-conductor of electricity and only a very poor conductor of those emotions that should be flowing from the living to the dead during flower-placing and flower tending cemetery visits. I would much rather look at a grave that hadn't been tended in years and thus was decorated only by Mother Nature (who doesn't do a bad job, by the way) than to look at one ringed by ersatz roses or other flowers placed there by someone whose sense of commitment to a departed loved one was non-renewable.

In the cemetery where most of my relatives and friends are buried, a township ordinance has just been passed which requires that all artificial decorations be removed by the first of October. That will help a lot, because I'll no longer have to avert my eyes when traveling past it in fall, winter, and early spring.

But I'm afraid I'll have to avert them again next summer unless—dare I believe it could happen?—this essay generates an epidemic of aversion to plastic flowers in cemeteries, and people will pay their respects with plants or, for special occasions, cut flowers, which, after they wither, blend into the ground rather than sully it with technicolor tawdriness. That, for me, is "a consummation devoutly to be wished."

# Berry Picking: I've Been Hooked All My Life

∾

"There isn't a train I wouldn't take, no matter where it's going," wrote Edna St. Vincent Millay in one of her poems. If I were her son, I suppose I'd be spending most of my free time running about the world on trains. But I am the son of another lady, who, though she doesn't write poetry, would have changed a couple of words in that line to read: "There isn't a berry I wouldn't pick, no matter where it's growing." And that is why so much of my summer is spent picking the berry of the moment.

Since it's not very likely that there is a berry-picking gene that can be passed on from generation to generation, this almost uncontrollable urge that I have to head for one berry patch or another in season can only be explained as a nurtural one.

When I was a kid, berry picking was an almost-necessity to satisfy a desire for sweet things that didn't disappear just because we were in the midst of the Great Depression. But my mother's enthusiasm for it convinced us all that we weren't working but having fun.

Late in the summer our whole family made three or four trips to the blueberry plains, where we filled milk pails and tubs with blueberries that grew in a profusion that is never likely to be matched again, in furrows plowed by the CCC boys as they reforested those sandy areas.

We stopped picking just long enough to eat lunch, which for us regularly consisted of fried chicken, home-made buns, and other goodies, which my mother magically prepared in between all the other daily chores that occupied her morning before we even started out on these expeditions. Later, homeward bound, we stopped at the Buckhorn Lodge for a bottle of pop or other refreshments.

Once home, our part of the operation was over, but my mother cleaned and then canned up to a hundred quarts of those berries so that come winter, however prosaic our meal may have been in those tough economic times, we partook of ambrosia at its conclusion. If it wasn't blueberries, it was raspberries, which we clambered over brush piles in timber slashings to find, and which my mother then canned and placed on shelves in our basement alongside their blueberry cousins.

Half a century has gone by since then, but I still heed the siren call of the blueberry plains, though I confess that I now do my raspberry picking in the friendly environs of Ray Trowbridge's magnificent raspberry patch in Ladoga, where he and I engage in a bit of reminiscing as we pick. I go to Ray's for the berries, but the conversation is a much-appreciated lagniappe. I picked sixty quarts there this year, canning forty of them and prevailing upon Judith, who's not into berries quite as much as I am, to make jam from some and freeze the rest.

The wild blueberry situation has changed from those years back in the thirties. There's been a pretty fair crop this year, but old-timers, yours truly among them, who remem-

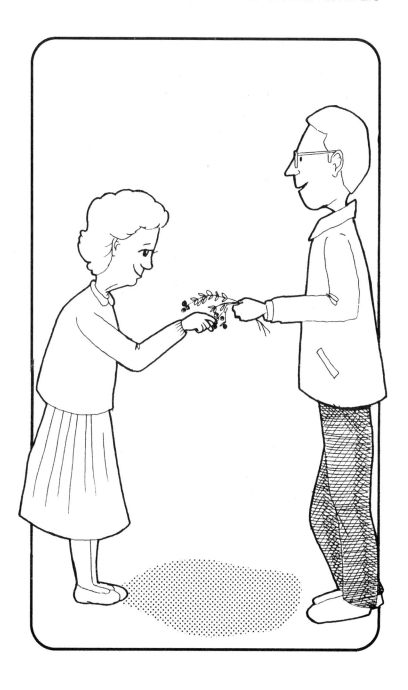

ber the way it used to be, despair of ever finding a true bonanza again and settle for a few quarts here and a few quarts there, for old time's sake.

My first hunt for the elusive blueberry this year took me to the plains in Alger County where I had picked them as a child. But the CCC boys had done their work well, and forests of pine now cover much of that area. Nevertheless, I found a spot and set out to fill my two-pound coffee can with them so that I would be assured of at least one fresh-blueberry pie this year.

Every sand fly, horsefly, deer fly, mosquito, and ant within a hundred yards of my picking spot found me before I was done, and a sudden thunder storm sent me away from the patch with my can not quite full. I must have been a pitiful sight when I got home and presented Judith with my treasure, because she almost immediately converted those berries into a pie, the first piece of which I ate while it was still warm enough to melt the big dip of vanilla ice cream I laid over the top of it, sending a liquid white to blend with a liquid blue and starting my own juices flowing doubletime.

I made a couple of more trips to pick blueberries after that. On one of them I found the largest bush I could, filled with ripe berries, and snapped it off so that I could present it to my mother. At age eighty-eight she has finally given up on blueberry picking herself, but she got that far-away look in her eye as she plucked those berries from that single bush with still-nimble fingers that had picked so many of those berries over the years, and I knew she accepted my offering as the thank you for her nurturing that I intended it to be.

# "Your Mother Should Have Taught You to Be Patient."

∽

It started out as a perfect day at the Red Fox Run golf course over at what used to be K.I. Sawyer AFB: none of the three other folks in my foursome was a better golfer than I (which, by the way, is not all that good); the morning sun had already warmed the air to a pleasant seventy degrees; and it looked as if we'd be off the first tee ten minutes ahead of our scheduled time.

But then I chanced to glance about a hundred yards ahead and to our left, where the women's tee was located, and noticed a couple of young ladies who seemed to be oblivious to our presence and to the absence of golfers on the green ahead of them. They laughed, swung at golf balls, which dribbled a few yards from them, retrieved the balls, laughed and chatted some more, and in other ways gave every indication of being in no hurry at all to begin their round.

I, all of a sudden, was, and I shouted something in their direction in what I thought was a firm but friendly manner that would get them moving. But it didn't. So I asked a course employee who was moving rental carts into position if he'd be kind enough to take a ride on one of those carts to inform those young ladies that we'd like to play through. This he did, and they moved, somewhat dejectedly it seemed to me from that distance, back to a bench on the tee to let us pass.

Their sudden change of mood generated my first pangs of regret for perhaps having been a bit brusque, and as I walked past them I stopped briefly and began to offer them a very short lesson on golf course etiquette. I expected them to be favorably impressed by my white hair, the kindly demeanor that I assumed for the occasion, and my avuncular advice. But they weren't. They listened for a moment before one of them touched me gently on the arm, looked me straight in the eye, and said: "Your mother should have taught you to be patient." I wish the printed page could convey the rhythm and tone she used in uttering those nine words. It was resigned, almost sad, but not disrespectful, conveying a "what is this older generation coming to" message to me.

Usually fairly adept at rejoinder and repartee, I was so stunned by that marvelous verbal zinger, delivered by someone barely out of high school, that the best I could come up with was: "You'll be happy to know that she is still alive and there is yet hope for me." But as I hurried to join the rest of my foursome, I felt myself growing smaller and smaller with every step I took away from those two obviously neophyte golfers. "Your mother should have taught you to be patient" kept rattling around in my head for the rest of that round with a disastrous impact on my score.

I hope that young lady gets to read this essay, because I'd like her to know that nobody before her had ever employed the English language to make a point any more effectively than she did with those nine words. I'd also like her to know that my mother, over the years, has been moderately successful in teaching me to be patient—but I do have these lapses, which I always regret afterwards. Finally, I'd like to tell that young lady that somewhere she and her friend should have been taught some basic golf course rules before stepping out onto one.

That brief encounter got me thinking about how people typically express their unhappiness with the behavior of others these days, which is, of course, all too often with violence. Batters charge pitchers who throw baseballs too close to their heads and try to "correct" them with their fists. Drivers step out of automobiles after a fender-bender accident and shoot other drivers dead.

Wouldn't it be nice if the next batter to get dusted off would charge to the mound, stop just in front of the pitcher, look him straight in the eye and say: "Your mother should have taught you not to throw baseballs at people's heads." And wouldn't it have been a welcome change of pace if the guy who started that near-riot at Madison Square Garden the other night had instead just walked up to the boxer who had been hitting his opponent below the belt and said to him: "Your mother should have taught you not to do that."

Yes, I know that such remarks place more of a burden on mothers than should be theirs, but if they work as well in boxing arenas and baseball stadiums as one did the other day on a local golf course, they ought to be given a try. This weekend Judith and I will be driving down-state in what I know will be heavy summer traffic. But this time I will NOT let loose a string of expletives in the direction of the first driver who does something foolish, because I have a strange feeling that the young lady I encountered the other day on the golf course will be riding in the back seat, at least in spirit, from where she will tap me on the shoulder and say: "Your mother should have taught you to be patient." I don't think I could handle another one of those for a while.

# Wild Animals and Me: Live and Let Live

∾

As I was writing a couple of weeks ago, I looked up from my word processor to see a very tiny mouse struggle across the carpeting in front of my desk and onto a ceramic-tiled area by the door. Apparently I had trapped its mother a couple of days earlier, and this poor mouse had no choice but to strike out on its own. For my part, I had no choice but to dispatch it, because baby mice grow up to be big ones, who then do things around the house that make their species fauna non grata.

Practically surrounded by woods, the basement of our house becomes a highly desirable lodging and foraging place for mice this time of the year, so I set out traps to discourage them (how's that for a euphemism!), feeling remorse for doing so only when I find one caught in such a way as to indicate a protracted death struggle.

But remorse is what I felt after I walked over to this baby mouse, waiting for me there on that ceramic tile, and stepped on it with my size ten Adidas sneakers. I picked this pathetic specimen of flattened fauna up by its tail, flushed it down the toilet, and then went back to my writing.

But my heart was no longer totally in my essay, though I hope I was able to conclude it without betraying my change in mood. The truth is that I have never gotten used to killing any of the wild animals that occasionally encroach upon my living space. Several years ago a large porcupine fell into the window well outside our basement and was unable to escape. It was quite likely the same one which had been gnawing on the bottom of our garage door, and I suppose I would have been justified in making it pay with its life for this offense.

But instead of going into the house for my shotgun, I went into the garage for a shovel and garbage can. I maneuvered the porcupine into the can with the shovel and then released it deep in the woods, from which it emerged several days later to resume its garage door gnawing, at which point I did go for my shotgun—but with the greatest reluctance.

I think I know whence comes this attitude toward the killing of animals. When I was about twelve, my father bought me my first gun, a single-shot .22 calibre rifle. After a brief course on gun safety he turned me loose with it, and I headed into the fields and woods around our place looking for something to kill.

Before long a woodchuck accommodated me by standing outside its hole on its hind legs looking at me curiously while I, trembling in anticipation of my first kill, squeezed off a shot in the general direction of the large target its exposed belly offered. The wounded animal fell to the ground and spent the next several minutes, which seemed like an eternity to me, pawing the air with all four legs while its life ebbed out of the rather insignificant hole that a small-calibre rifle makes.

I did not have the presence of mind to administer the

coup de grace from close up, but just stood there feeling miserable and very, very guilty. Then I went directly home to write the first poem of my life in tribute to that departed woodchuck.

It was doggerel, of course, but in the depths of my despair and remorse it seemed like heavy and profound poetry at the time. Half a century later I can still remember its closing lines: "If God made the world for me and you, He must have made it for the woodchuck, too..." Kind of corny, even for a twelve-year-old, but, though I would express that sentiment in more sophisticated ways as I grew older, its essence hasn't changed much for me over the years.

That is why a huge bank beaver who moved in with us more than two years ago is still alive. After trying to build a dam for several months, which I broke down every morning, he settled for some sort of domicile off in the tag elders, and now he swims about our pond either oblivious to me or aware somehow that I represent no danger to him.

Beavers have become quite a nuisance on Dexter Creek in recent years, so my friends doubtless make more sense than I when they tell me that I should shoot every one I see in the interest of saving the Dexter as a prime trout stream. But I won't do that because rattling around in my head for all these years is a line of poetry written by a twelve-year-old boy.

So I'll just honor my unwritten joint tenancy agreement with most of the animal kingdom and leave the responsibility for keeping it under control to someone else. Mice, for the record, shall continue to be excluded from that agreement.

# Rule Benders Depend upon Rule Keepers

∽

I was sitting at the airport in Amsterdam waiting to return home from one of those vacations I take to Europe every three or four years to help keep life interesting when the public address system announced that it was time for me and four hundred fellow travelers to board the 747 that was to fly us to Minneapolis.

I started to obey the directive when one of my companions said that I was foolish to do so, explaining that because we all had assigned seats we shouldn't be standing in line and inching forward at a snail's pace but should wait instead for everyone else to board and then walk leisurely but quickly to our seats.

He announced proudly that this was what he always did, and I succumbed just that one time to his logic. But I wasn't comfortable doing so because I was aware that the rest of the passengers had to follow instructions in order for us to get away with not doing so.

To me what we were doing was a form of exploitation of those four hundred others. That realization and the vision of what might have happened if they all decided to wait for someone else to board first has kept me from repeating that ploy on the several flights I have taken since.

It occurs to me now that a valid generalization can be drawn from the experience: people can bend the rules and ignore instructions to convenience themselves only when the general public does not, and that public is, in a sense, subsidizing and being victimized by this necessarily small minority.

Another example: handicapped parking spots. I almost never shop at the grocery store without seeing at least one car without a handicapped sticker or license parked in one of those spots. But because most of us wouldn't think of violating the law in this regard, the drivers of those cars get away with it much of the time and probably think of themselves as being smarter than the rest of us for doing so. Most rule benders and instruction ignorers seem to perceive themselves this way, and few think that their actions constitute exploitation and selfishness—but they do.

A few weeks ago I watched a customer in a store downstate remove from his shopping cart a can of motor oil and lay it in between a couple of piles of blue jeans. Not much of a crime, I know, in a place where someone was probably stealing a car from the store's parking lot at that very moment. But his act took money out of my pocket and yours because the manager of that store had to employ someone to take that can of oil and other items of intentionally misplaced merchandise to their proper locations. You may be sure that that employee's wages show up in the price of every item in the store, however minutely.

More important, if the majority of customers behaved the way this one did, most department stores and supermarkets would be in a constant state of chaos, and we would have to return to the way it was in the old days, when customers stood on one side of a counter and pointed to items which would then be brought to them by a clerk.

I know what I'm writing about today is not a "biggie," but I think it's worth reminding readers that our world works at least reasonably well because most of us are willing to go along with rules for a lot of little things. So the next time you're inclined to engage in conversation with your companion in a theater while the movie's in progress, consider what would happen if everyone else did so at the same time. In fact, think about that whenever you're about to do something that's "against the rules."

Of course, because there are a good many incompetents among the rule makers of the world and because some rules don't deserve to be adhered to, you should always stand ready to challenge directives which are patently absurd, but do so aggressively and up front. And if your challenge is unsuccessful, just shrug your shoulders and go along the next time—for the good of the order. Who knows, maybe the rest of the world is right on this one.

# Olga Smith—A Jump Ahead of Most of Us

∾

Visiting folks in the hospital is something I do considerably more often now than I did twenty years ago because so many of my friends and relatives are at the maintenance and repair stage of their lives. But the repairs are usually things like pacemaker implants, heart by-pass surgery, "roto rooter" prostate procedures, etc. And, of course, the conditions which require those repairs are usually beyond the control of people undergoing them.

But Olga Smith, aged seventy, did not have to jump out of an airplane a few weeks ago, and had she not opted to do so, she wouldn't have wound up in Marquette General Hospital with a fractured hip. One of the first things she told me when I dropped in on her there was that she had decided to make that fateful parachute jump because she wanted to prove to herself and other septuagenarians that they weren't condemned to spend the rest of their lives launching themselves into and out of nothing more exciting than reclining chairs, and bailing out of an airplane seemed like a good way to demonstrate that.

What amazed me was that the unfortunate result of this adventure did not deter her for a moment from continuing to think that it was a great idea. I was with her for at least ten minutes before she got around to talking about the bad part at all, because she was anxious to tell me about the good stuff that preceded it. A few details about the fracture were tacked on to her narrative of the event as a sort of afterthought.

The look of pride on her face as she spoke illustrated to me, more forcefully than it's ever been done before, that the old song was right: "You've got to accentuate the positive, eliminate the negative..." Olga told me first about the thrill she felt in realizing that she had leaped out of the plane with considerably less trepidation than she had anticipated and certainly less than she observed in a couple of other first-timers who went out ahead of her.

She spoke of how well she followed the orders about which shroud line to pull as they were radioed to her by her instructor—right up until she was within a few feet of being back down, when she must have pulled on one just a tad too much, which caused her to hit the ground at more of an angle than she should have. "Oh, well, those things happen" was her obvious attitude, and, broken hip be damned, she was glad she had made that jump.

Then she went back to describing the good parts once more, directing my attention, somewhere along the line, to a certificate hanging on the wall of her hospital room, one that said she had successfully completed her first jump. I found it remarkable that the kind of serious injury she suffered at the end of it may have marred her body a bit but didn't mar the meaning of "success" one iota, either on that certificate or in her mind.

It occurred to me that most folks in the same situation would have seen the experience as a failure and would have said so over and over again: "How stupid I was to do that...how could I have been so foolish...I should have acted my age... now I'll probably be crippled for the rest of my life..." and on and on—each assertion helping to forge a permanent self image of failure.

But I like the way Olga handled it, and though you may be sure this groundling will never launch himself out of an airplane door unless that plane is parked at an airport, I may do something else that produces the equivalent of a broken hip at its terminus. When I do, I hope that I, too, will have the good sense to focus on all the good stuff that went before it and see success where the pessimist would see failure.

It really is true: the perception of an event is much more significant than the event itself. One person plants a field of beans that is later destroyed by frost and remembers only the blackened dead plants—and his failure as a gardener. Another recalls the thrill of seeing the young plants pop from the brown earth and the beautiful straight lines of green they formed against it.

A bit corny? Perhaps, but we all know which of those gardeners is more likely to keep on gardening—or at least which one is going to be happier at it. As for Olga, just before I left, I asked her if she was likely to try parachute jumping again. Wistfully, she said no—after all, she's a realist as well as a dreamer. But the twinkle in her eye told me that she had a couple of other things in mind. If her bones are as healthy as her spirit, she's probably at them by now.

# I'll Stick to Gambling with Nature

∾

It was eleven o'clock on a beautiful April morning. I had begun my day early with a trip to Munising to put the finishing touches on *Alger Footprints*, a historical society newsletter which I edit. That beautiful eight-mile stretch of M94 which I had mentioned in a recent column on spring colors had made me feel so lucky to be living in the central U.P. that none of the frustrations awaiting me at my printer's office could shake the euphoria just generated.

My work there done, I headed west along M 28 toward Marquette. When I got to the top of the hill just outside of town I looked to my right out at Munising Bay, its waters matching, and even surpassing, the blueness of the sky above it. Chunks of snow-ice, dazzling white, punctuated the blue of the water, and off in the distance I could just make out Pictured Rocks.

I was in the midst of a natural U.P. high! This is what my beloved peninsula is all about, I thought to myself. But a huge sign inviting passersby to stop at a casino just a couple of miles down the road brought me down from my high to the sad realization that, more and more, the U.P. is also about something else these days.

I consoled myself with the thought that at that hour of the day surely no one would choose the interior of a gambling casino made bright only by the flashing lights of slot machines—not when the brightness that counts was so abundantly available outdoors. Wrong! When I got to the place, I counted at least two dozen vehicles alongside it— so much for that idea.

Thirty miles down the highway good feelings slowly regenerated by countless scenes of spectacular Lake Superior beauty were once more dashed by a sign, this one luring gamblers to the second casino on M28 between Marquette and Munising.

Would I have reacted differently if I had encountered these signs on a gloomy day (we've had plenty of those this spring) along the barren Seney stretch of the same highway, in the middle of a huge swamp? Maybe—a little. But I did not feel comfortable when the first casino made its appearance in the U.P., and I feel even less so every time I read about a new one coming on line or an existing one expanding to "serve" more people.

I suspect my attitude is colored somewhat by my first experience with gambling, when I was only fourteen. One-armed bandits existed back then but were not available to me. Punchboards were, however, and as I ate a hamburger at a local eatery one day, its proprietor waved one of those boards under my nose and suggested that it represented an "easy way to pick up a couple of bucks."

I had two quarters left over from my hamburger transaction, so I said: "Why not." If you're under fifty you probably don't even know what a punchboard is, so let me explain: little slips of paper, accordion pleated, are stuck into small holes in a board. For a given sum of money—a quarter in this case—the purchaser pushes one of those slips of paper out of the hole with an instrument called a punch and then unfolds it to see if he's won anything.

The board I played was based upon playing cards, with an ace being worth $25. My first quarter yielded nothing, but my second, wonder of wonders, produced an ace of spades. The proprietor paid me off and then said—I suspect there was a gleam in his eye—"You know, there are four aces in every deck. You want to try your luck again?"

Of course I did, and I walked out of that restaurant twenty minutes later with only the two quarters I had started with. I have no idea what belated good sense prevented me from spending those, too. Just writing about the experience still produces that terrible feeling in the pit of my stomach that dominated every minute of my day for at least a week as I contemplated the great fortune that I had held in my hand for those brief moments.

Bear in mind that when I was fourteen $25 would buy a brand new bicycle with horn, headlights, etc. At the time I was sharing a girls' bike, bought used by my father for my older sister. I won't tell you all the other things it would have bought—I think you get the picture.

At any rate that one experience has colored my attitude toward gambling ever since, with reinforcement coming from half a dozen other come-up-empty gambling fiascoes as a young adult. I have since listened to friends tell me of similar experiences. There's something in the psychology of gambling that has folks plowing back their "profits" in hopes of hitting jackpots that most never do—much to the joy and real profit of casino operators.

To head off cries of "Hypocrite!" from my acquaintances, I confess to buying an occasional lottery ticket. I also participated, when I was teaching, in the annual Super Bowl pool, once having $250 within my grasp when, with only two seconds left in the quarter, my numbers (7-0)

were sure winners as soon as the extra point was kicked—
it wasn't!

And about every two weeks I get together with the boys
for what we euphemistically refer to as "choir practice,"
where my four of a kind is all too often beaten out by a
straight flush.

I think that gambling, confined to the activities listed
immediately above, is generally a harmless pursuit. But
there's some evidence that casino gambling often is not,
either for the participants or the folks living in communi-
ties where it takes place.

I was happier when gamblers were loaded into air-
planes and flown off to Las Vegas to do their thing so that
the rest of us could do ours in the fields, forests, lakes, and
streams so abundantly available to us up here—in sunlight
rather than under the garish glow of slot machines.

# The Child Is Father to the Man!

∾

Several weeks ago we entertained house guests who had two small children. When one of those kids behaved badly, her mother's response was: "I think she's been watching too many sit-coms on television." In saying this she was reflecting a commonly held opinion (and, I think, an accurate one) that the behavior of people as they are portrayed on TV in those shows and other types impacts upon those watching them, whatever their age.

I haven't been much of a fan of TV situation comedies lately because, with only a couple of exceptions, they have been going downhill steadily since the days of the "Andy Griffith" and "Mary Tyler Moore" shows. But I've watched enough with kids of various ages in those programs (they seem to be almost de rigueur in such comedies these days) to realize that if real-life kids are picking up on half of the bad examples they're exposed to on the tube, we're in serious trouble in that department.

TV kids did not always set bad examples. The first one

I had much television contact with was Opie from the "Andy Griffith" show. He was predictably cute—television kids are either uncommonly attractive or swamp ugly (rare), but he behaved like a boy who had read the same rule book I had when I was growing up.

He talked to adults, yes, but he never talked back to them. And when he came close to doing so he was always stopped in his tracks by a "That'll be enough now, Opie," from his father, to which his response was invariably "Yes, sir." And he generally fessed up to wrongdoings, which in his case were never more than peccadilloes.

We didn't have television to guide us in my childhood (for which I am grateful) but most of us behaved more like Opie than his counterparts on TV today. I remember once when I was about nine years old going home to my father, opening up my grubby little hand to expose an equally grubby penny, and announcing to him that I had earned it on the playground at school. When he questioned me for particulars, it didn't even occur to me not to tell him that one of the older boys had given it to me for beating up on another kid in my class.

The outcome of that episode was never in doubt. My dad handed me his jackknife and sent me outside to cut a switch of a size appropriate to the punishment I deserved and rejected several before I bowed to the inevitable—literally. My dad was, and is, a kind man but he understood his role as teacher, and I learned early that there are right ways and wrong ways to earn money.

I haven't watched anything comparable to that episode on TV, but I've seen a lot of parents standing in front of locked doors pleading with their kids to let them in. And I've watched kids throw temper tantrums and get the desired results from them. I've endured the antics of smart alecks who had to have the last word and who were over-impressed by their own cuteness. Worst of all, I've been subjected to bargaining sessions in which children have cut deals that made their parents look ridiculous.

I don't believe in censorship of the media, not because the concept is necessarily bad, but because I don't trust anyone to do the job the way I think it should be done, and in the past it has always created its own excesses. But I certainly don't buy into the excuse most TV program producers offer: that what they are giving us reflects life as it is today. The TV fare produced under that rationale is helping to hasten the downward spiral of society to who knows where.

It may be that society is too far out of control to be returned to some kind of equilibrium. But if it's going to happen, starting with our children seems like a good idea.

And if many really are behaving like Roseanne's brats, why can't television offer up a few more good role models. I'm quite sure that there are some adults out there today who turned out better because they had shows like "Andy Griffith" to watch instead of "Roseanne." And "The Waltons," as Pollyannish as that program sometimes was, offered viewers many examples of the way family members ought to interact with each other.

I can't argue against the notion that art does indeed imitate life. But every day we see plenty of evidence of where that has gotten us. Maybe it's time for the media to reverse the nouns in the slogan they've been using to defend themselves and to give us a little more of the kind of art that life could imitate without destroying itself.

# The Women I Married

∾

I'm married to two Judith Bartols, both very fascinating women whom I dearly love. I put the one who sits across the kitchen table from me three times a day, the one with whom I play Scrabble on Wednesday and Sunday evenings (unless she tells me that she has a headache) on a bus to Kalamazoo ten days ago.

But I had hardly returned home from the ride to the bus station when the other one began to materialize in my mind and heart, the one who "walks in beauty like the night of cloudless climes and starry skies, and all that's best of dark and light meet in her aspect and her eyes" (Byron, in case you're wondering).

It's an interesting process, this idealization of one's mate in his/her absence. The one I've been married to for forty-three years measures up pretty well when we're together, I'm happy to say, and I've always considered myself a very lucky guy. But she sometimes tells me to comb my hair, shave, put on a clean shirt, or do other things that suggest she doesn't find me perfect in whatever form I present myself to her. And she gives me lists of things around the place that need doing and nudges me from time to see that they get done.

When we travel by car she loses herself in a book immediately and is oblivious to the scenery around her, responding only with a "mm-hmm" when I try to call attention to something that she ought to look up at. At home, she corrals the television set to do her morning video exercise when I want to watch the "Today" show.....AND SHE HAS AN AUDIO TAPE LABELED "JUDITH'S FAVORITE SONGS," WHICH SHE PLAYS ALMOST EVERY DAY AND WHICH CONTAINS A SONG THAT STARTS WITH "I AM WOMAN, HEAR ME ROAR..........."

But by the third day of her absence that Judith began to disappear from my memory screen to be replaced by the one I got my first glimpse of in January of 1952 as I stood at the second floor railing of old Kaye Hall at NMU looking down at new mid-year enrollees. Believe it or not, I pronounced her "the one" at that very moment and began my campaign to win her hand. It was then that the images I always return to in her absence began to pile up: tender goodnights at the Carey Hall entrance, formal dances at the Lee Hall Ballroom, drives out to standard lovers' lanes of that time, and, of course, on August 6th, 1953, the most beautiful image of all: Judith coming down the aisle of the First Presbyterian Church in Ishpeming with the heavy rain that had drenched the wedding guests and us as we entered coming down so hard still that we could hear it on the roof during the wedding ceremony. Rain can never be a bad omen for me.

By the seventh day nothing was left of the Judith that I got to know in the important, but not always romantic ways folks get to know each other through forty-three years of marriage, and I expected the one I went to meet at the bus station at 1:15 A.M. three days ago to float out of that bus without her feet touching the ground, her path to me lit by an aura surrounding her.

It wasn't quite that way, but she looked great, and the reunion was worth the loneliness. True, she went to work to re-establish the other Judith, albeit unconsciously, the very next day when she re-arranged the kitchen more to her liking, removing the milk carton which I have always considered such a convenient receptacle for potato peelings, egg shells, left-over food, etc. and which I planned to take to the garbage can only when odors emanating from it signaled to me that bacterial life was going on inside it. We have fought the milk carton battle ever since the early days of our marriage, but I have never won it.

Last night as we sat in our newly-built sun porch, with a nice fire in the glass-fronted wood stove and all the windows in place to keep out the cool evening air, she began to fan herself with a book—which she is never without—and I knew that she would soon rise to her full height of 5' 2" and remove a window only slightly shorter than she and almost as heavy, remarking as she did so that she just HAD to have some fresh air.

We are never comfortable at the same temperature, but that was all right last night because both of my images of Judith were in perfect balance in my eyes and heart then, and SHE seemed more tolerant of the Frank who starts turning into an icicle at temperatures that make her sweat. We have been very fortunate in that before petty annoyances turn into major aggravations, one or the other of us has occasion to depart the premises for a few days, and in our separation we learn how much we love to be together.

# Sorry, Summer, You Lost Out Again

∾

I suppose some kind of case could be made for summer as the best of the four seasons, but it's not going to be made by me. On my list it will probably come in dead last this year. Yes, it's the season when I play most of my golf, but I haven't been doing it well enough lately to give summer any brownie points on that account. To make matters worse, this past Monday, as I waited for my tee time at the Red Fox Run golf course at K.I. Sawyer, I made the mistake of hitting a bucket of balls on the driving range there.

Lately I've been in the habit of saying: "I know I'm not one of the big stickers. I'm satisfied if I can just get my drives out there about two hundred yards." Well, honest man that I am, I won't be saying it any more—at least not until I can forget my experience that day. You see, no matter how mightily I swung, no matter how loudly I grunted during that swing, and no matter how well I followed through, kept my head down, etc. my drives were dropping between the 150-yard and 200-yard markers. Two of them even collided with the first of those markers on their way down just to embarrass me further.

I've used gardening in past years to boost summer's rating a bit, but I made a second mistake just this morning when I checked out the garden of my friend, Louis Laurich, who lives three miles south of us. Until I saw his, mine could have earned enough points to get summer out of the seasonal cellar. But where some of his cucumbers are already beginning to blossom, my pitiful plants are just now making their appearance. And the size of his cabbage plants suggests that he will be eating garden cole slaw when I'm still coaxing my cabbages to get ahead (pun intended).

I'll always enjoy my garden, of course, and I'm not ashamed of this year's version. I'm also quite sure that by summer's end both my friend and I will be giving away considerably more garden produce than we'll be eating. But recent disappointments in gardening and golf have removed what little shine summer ever has for me. Speaking of shine, I'm continually being warned to keep out of it when it's produced by the sun unless I smear myself with a minimum of two ounces of No. 15 sun screen to prevent the skin cancer that will otherwise surely get me.

What has put summer beyond the pale again, however, has been the serial attack of insects. I don't know why I should be surprised; it's an annual feast—for the insects, that is. But somehow I manage to blot most of it from my memory over the winter and have to be reintroduced to the horrors of that sequential onslaught each summer.

Depending upon where a particular person has spent the past six weeks, this either has or has not been the worst bug year since (you name the year). My own experience places it about in the middle on the misery scale. But I am once again unhappily impressed by the scheduled arrival and departure of these insectile torturers. No species ever leaves until its replacement is in place, its biting equipment well sharpened, orders in hand to take no prisoners and show no mercy.

To those of you who mostly stay indoors and thus have been getting stung only by the internet and telemarketing scams so far this season, let me give a run-down of the way it goes. Black flies are the first on the scene. Small but with a decidedly large, welt-raising bite, they are not discouraged by insect repellants but actually seem to thrive on them. Their victims are easily identified by a line of black-fly-produced blotches on their heads which show the point where the caps designed to protect them end and their bare skin begins.

Next come mosquitoes, so numerous sometimes that they are said to come in clouds. Only the females suck our blood, but there are at least a dozen of that sex for every square inch of exposed human flesh available to them so there's more than enough mosquito misery to go around right through mid-summer, when the stagnant pools of water they need to breed have pretty much dried up. Mosquitoes can be kept at bay by good repellants, though, so they are less of a problem than the other species.

But the main attack force, composed of deer flies, sand flies, and the B 52s of the biting insect force, horseflies, swoop down on any target of opportunity during all of July and August. The tenacity of deer flies is legendary and their bites formidable. I have resorted to netting sometimes to protect myself when I weed my garden, but it obstructs my vision so much that I wind up pulling up more vegetables than weeds, so I cast it aside and resign myself to being bitten until I can stand it no more.

If my dog Jake could talk, I know he would tell me not to forget wood ticks, which plague him more than me but are enough of a nuisance to both of us. I'm reluctant to

pet him during the summer because just about every time I do my hand encounters a tick, swollen to kidney bean size by Jake's blood. I'll spare you the unpleasant details of the removal of those offensive creatures. A couple of weeks ago I resorted to a flea and tick collar for Jake, which so far seems to be at least partially effective.

Toward the end of August, when all of the above-mentioned species are on the wane, ground wasps, paper wasps, and hornets are at their nastiest. An attack from them on any given day outdoors is not a certainty, but the prospect of one gives me pause, especially so because I have developed an allergy to their stings and really should carry an anti-venom kit with me at all times.

So let summer insects do their damnedest. I've survived them thus far and look forward to doing so for another decade or so. But two months from now I expect to be shouting: "Up and autumn!" with a big smile of greeting on my face for the season which—you guessed it—has always been number one on my list.

# Domestic Redundancy=Economic Salvation

∾

The business page of my newspaper tells me that our economy is humming along nicely for the moment. Cars and pickups and other big ticket items are selling quite briskly, and unemployment is down dramatically. But on that same page there's an item about companies "leaning down" in their attempts to achieve a satisfactory profit.

These companies are also burning the midnight oil as they try to stay one jump ahead of the competition by developing high resolution television sets, ultra-something telephone systems, super computers that fit into the palm of one's hand, and a lot of other technological wonders that they hope to entice us to buy.

Well, I'm quite happy with my TV, phone, and word processor, thank you, so no matter what they come up with along those lines I'm not likely to help keep the economy lively by buying replacements for them. But I do want to help, and I think I've come up with a way I can that won't strain my budget too much and will make life a little easier for me at the same time.

I've been hearing and reading a lot lately about redundancy in our space program and the technology it has spawned. The term simply means that there are backup everythings on a spacecraft that can be called into play when the originals malfunction. Now here's my idea: if we would build a little of that same redundancy into our domestic lives we could keep employment levels high.

This process doesn't have to be anything complicated and expensive, and most of the time it wouldn't be dealing with the problem of malfunctions but rather with the simple disappearance of things in and about the home from those places where we expect to find them whenever we need them. If we just had two, three, or maybe even half a dozen of those items, we'd surely always be able to lay our hands on one without looking too long for it.

I came up with this jewel of an idea just yesterday, when I spent at least fifteen minutes searching for a roll of electrical tape that I needed for a switch replacement job. Eventually I located it in one of six likely places, and it occurred to me that if I had kept a roll of that tape in each of those spots, I could have found one in a minute or less and saved myself a good deal of stress at the same time. If five extra rolls of electrical tape were to be added to the supply in every household where there is a handyman about the place who is likely to need one (most guys I know claim to be handymen), just think of the economic impact on those industries that manufacture such tape.

In order to implement such a redundancy plan, we must first make up a list of items to place on it. In addition to those rolls of tape, here are some other things that would go on mine: screwdrivers, jackknives, pliers, rolls of string, fingernail clippers, combs, ballpoint pens, claw hammers, can openers, measuring tapes—and that's just for starters.

In addition to giving the economy a boost, establishing redundancy with items of this kind would be an environmentally friendly activity because it is a given that such objects continue to disappear, never to show up again to create an eventual disposal problem. Where they go I've never been able to figure out. Maybe they simply disintegrate into their constituent elements after a time.

Once in a while they do pop up again to create a problem of oversupply but that's almost always a temporary phenomenon. Even before I hatched this ingenious plan I attempted to achieve adequate redundancy with one of the items on the above list: screwdrivers. I bought a set (they almost always come in sets these days) to put in each of three locations—my basement, workshop, and garage—and then observed as they gradually disappeared from the racks I provided for them. I think now that I'll have to add a set to keep in one of the drawers in our kitchen cabinetry right next to the measuring spoons (aha! another item for my list).

Once all of those screwdrivers re-appeared at the same time to fill up those racks, plus one from who knows where. That made me nervous. But I just jammed that extra one in with one of its fellows and slammed the cabinet door on it. When I checked again a few days later it had obligingly disappeared.

One caveat: I think my plan should be limited to the domestic scene. Employed in the professional and industrial sector, it might have the opposite effect of the one intended. If carpenters, electricians, auto mechanics, doctors, dentists, beauticians, etc. kept too many of the tools of their trade close at hand, they might spend so much less time zigging and zagging about their workplaces looking for calipers, scalpels, and gauze that they'd finish their work too soon and thus throw our always fragile economy into a deep recession.

I'll leave it to others to worry about that one while I give the economy the only kind of boost that I can within my budget by going over to the hardware store for five rolls of electrical tape.

# Fourth of July, 1939: A Ritual Remembered

∾

The sun has just barely risen over the treetops east of our home, a direction in which my ears and those of my brother Don are cocked as we stand outside to receive the full auditory impact of a series of explosions which we know are about to occur, just as they have every year on this date for as long as we can remember, which isn't very long, because I am only ten and Don had his ninth birthday only three days ago. Last year we heard those same explosions muffled by the walls of our house, and we want to be closer to the action this time around.

The source of those blasts is the Matt Bell residence, a quarter of a mile due east of our place, from where Matt arouses late sleepers—there aren't many of them in this farming community—and announces to others like my brother and me, the farmers doing their barn chores, and the housewives preparing breakfast, that the Fourth of July celebration has "officially" begun.

We are as excited about the listening as we presume

Matt to be about the detonating, and when it happens we're convinced that we can feel a rush of air past our faces from the blasts, though that is not possible across the quarter-mile of woods and swamp that separates our two places.

Traunik is a quiet community on this Independence Day, and the sound of half a dozen dynamite explosions is "quite something." Ironically, at least a dozen young men within earshot of those ritual explosions will be hearing others, those of World War II, all too soon, and two will not return from that conflict.

But we don't know about any of that yet, though my parents have been reading in the newspaper about some dictator in Germany named Hitler, and their brows furrow in worry when they talk about our many relatives in Slovenia. For Don and me Matt's dynamite blasts are not a portent of bad times but a signal to go into the house for a little flag that is carefully and respectfully wrapped around its three-foot staff, stored in a safe place, and brought out on two occasions annually: Memorial Day (we call it "Decoration Day") and the Fourth of July.

We march down our long gravel driveway pretending we are flag bearers in a military unit, like those we've seen in pictures of Revolutionary War and Civil War soldiers going into action, and we stop at our gate post, where two fence staples, set at an angle by my father years ago and quite rusty now, wait to receive the flag. This is an era when fences are still needed to keep cows out if one is not a dairy farmer and to keep them in if one is, so there are fence posts available in front of everybody's house, at most of which the same ritual is occurring.

Conspicuous consumption is being held at bay during this time of the Great Depression, and there is no showing off as far as flag size is concerned, at least not on the part of our neighbors on either side, which is about as much of

the world as we have much awareness of. But the flags are all cleaned and well cared for. None show signs of having been left out in the weather. The ends of none are tattered from long exposure to Upper Peninsula winds.

We all know the rules relating to flag display and storage, having been taught them through precept and the example of those about us. I feel a little guilty if I ever let the cloth of the flag touch the ground as I take it down the driveway. Years later, when the second war "to end all wars" is almost ancient history, flag rules and others we are living by now will be ignored, or even scoffed at.

Flags will be nailed to the fronts of buildings, there to remain until they rot. Or they will hang from their staffs day and night, whether a light is trained on them or not. Gas station owners will compete with each other to see who can hoist the largest one. There will be several within an hour's drive of our village large enough to blanket an average house. And flags will be emblazoned on T-shirts, tennis shoes, and countless other manufactured products.

Ironically, a society that will tolerate this kind of abuse of the flag will become collectively incensed by folks who publicly burn it to protest some things done in its name during what will come to be known as the Viet Nam era.

But this is 1939, and after the Fourth of July celebration in Trenary, followed by a family picnic, maybe, at a nearby lake, which will feature fried chicken that no one in the world makes as well as my mother, Don and I will take another walk down that long driveway as darkness descends to gently disengage our flag from the staples which held it in place all day, roll it up around that little flag staff, and return it to its place of honor for another eleven months.

Then, if we're lucky, we'll be able to talk our parents into driving us five miles south to Trenary again in our almost-new 1936 Chevrolet so that we can end our day as we had begun it, listening to another series of explosions, these generated by fireworks, which I hope will still be around for folks to enjoy far into the future—maybe even in 1995!

# Why Can't You Smile, Mr. Police Officer?

∾

I had just been told that the odor inside the passenger compartment of my car was caused by a blown intake manifold seal, which it would cost me over $300 to have replaced, this information coming on the heels of an estimate of $100 or more to bring my word processor back up to snuff. I engaged in the two diagnostic errands which produced those numbers immediately after my fifth straight disastrous bowling session over at the Eastwood Lanes in Marquette, where I had to endure the pity of several men---and women---a number of years my senior who were knocking down fifty or more pins per game than I.

Finally homeward bound for a quick meal before heading on to Munising for a historical society meeting, why was I, after all this misery, sitting in my car on the shoulder of U.S. 41 just outside of Harvey with a speeding citation in my hand, feeling no anger toward the police officer who had, unknowingly of course, really piled it on for me last Monday afternoon?

Part of the answer can be found in the proverb: "As the twig is bent so the tree will grow." This particular twig grew up in such awe of the Michigan State Police that the sixty-four-year-old tree is still conditioned to respond with respect and acceptance to the judgment of any of its officers, even that of the fresh-out-of-the-academy one who had handed me the ticket, who ought to have seen that the white-haired old guy hurrying home to the bosom of his family was generally an upstanding, law-abiding citizen, who would have been eternally grateful for a warning instead of a ticket.

My first run-in with the law occurred when I was at the impressionable age of ten, when I sicced my dog Jack, a diminutive terrier with a fighting spirit, on a brakeman for the Soo Line Railroad, which ran past our house. I meant nothing bad by it really because I assumed that Jack's aggressiveness was limited to woodchucks, skunks, and porcupines, and I had no idea that calves, when attached to railroad trainmen were also fair game for him.

But he did my bidding---or should I say "biting"--- producing a wound in said brakeman which required medical attention and resulted in a visit by two state police officers, who directed my parents to confine my dog for ten days so that he could be observed for signs of rabies.

I won't even try to describe my emotions as I watched that automotive symbol of authority come up our long driveway and disgorge two human symbols, who marched purposefully and unsmilingly up to the only adult on the premises at the time, my mother, with the dog confinement order.

It must be remembered that back in those days cars and officers tended to be more conspicuously accoutered than they are today and contrasted more dramatically with the man and car on the street. The Michigan State Police logo was emblazoned large on police car doors and, if memory serves me well, a wide ribbon was painted diagonally the entire length of the car to call even more attention to that logo.

The uniforms of the officers made them look larger than life, especially from the upward angle that I viewed them as I cowered in the shadow of their magnificent hats and looked straight on at their shiny leather Sam Browne gun belts. Their high boots were similarly shiny. Everything, including their badges and cleanly-shaven faces, was in shiny but somber harmony, and I could practically see an aura surrounding them as they issued their by-the-book orders to my mother.

That early attitude of awe and respect was imprinted in me so indelibly that even now I find it difficult to say anything critical about a police officer. But I hope I will be forgiven if I suggest that there are some situations in which one of them might utter something other than "May I see your driver's license, please," as his opening remark to folks he has just pulled over. That always rattles me and causes me to fumble through every compartment of my billfold before coming up with the requested item.

Even doctors and dentists smile and exchange a few pleasantries with their patients before performing surgery on them. May I suggest to "my" police officer and any others who might read this that a frivolous comment or two, with an accompanying smile, would help to break the ice in these encounters. Even the hackneyed "Where's the fire?" opener would have helped in my case because it would have signaled the officer's intent and would not have had me, momentarily, thinking that I was being pulled over to be issued a "good citizen" award for using a flashing-headlights signal to get other drivers to turn on their lights, an act which I had performed just seconds before being pulled over.

Oh, well, maybe next time. In the meantime, Mr. Police

Officer, I forgive you---because that's the way I was brought up.

# The Big City Can Be Friendly

∾

All right, I recently wrote an essay in tribute to small-town friendliness, which contained criticism of big cities as unfriendly, impersonal places. When this essay appeared as a newspaper column it generated a couple of letters from folks who had moved from one of those big cities to the Upper Peninsula and found us Yoopers anything but the kind of warm-hearted, caring persons I described.

Maybe those critics just haven't been up here long enough to really get to know us, but they got me thinking about the issue a bit more, and even though I still believe that the stereotype I presented was valid, it, like most generalizations, leaks enough to warrant caution on the part of the believer.

This was brought home to me dramatically this past weekend when I spent two days in Chicago. Unbeknownst to me, a young man from Germany, who was touring the United States and was to be our house guest as soon as I returned from my trip, was there at the same time. A brief

I THOUGHT YOU'D NEVER ASK!

outline of our separate activities in that city will help explain why this was a learning experience for me.

I drove downtown directly to Michigan Avenue, which is the only part of "the Loop" that I feel comfortable and safe in. Eschewing a couple of parking lots on the south part of that avenue, where parking was relatively inexpensive but the area a bit seamy, I chose the parking ramp in the John Hancock Building—and shelled out $11 for the privilege of parking there for my five-hour downtown stay.

After doing some window shopping at Nieman-Marcus and Saks Fifth Avenue—the only kind of shopping I could afford in stores that featured neckties for $100 or more—I decided to visit the Shedd Aquarium. Not willing to risk whatever parking problem might exist there, I took a taxi ($7 each way). I won't detail the rest of my activities that day, but suffice it to say that I did all the "safe" things, all the while assuming that it would be pointless and maybe even dangerous to ask for directions or any other assistance.

My German friend, on the other hand, completely unencumbered by any preconceived notions about the safety of travel in the big city, drove directly to the University of Chicago in his rented car. A graduate student himself, he said he always sought out universities in the cities he visited. Those of you who know Chicago also know that the University is a small oasis of education surrounded by an environment that most of us wouldn't walk or drive through in broad daylight, much less late in the evening when he did.

But he negotiated it without incident and made contact with folks there who had some authority over university housing and who offered him free lodgings on campus for three days.

The next day he drove to Michigan Avenue, too, because he was familiar with the reputation of "the magnificent mile" and wanted to see it for himself. But he did-n't park at the John Hancock. Instead, he prevailed upon a guy at the fire station near Water Tower Place to let him park his car there while he looked around.

On Sunday, as he continued his tour of the city, he noticed very heavy traffic around Soldier Field, so he pulled his car up to an area where many taxis were parked and inquired as to the reason for all those cars. When he was told a Bears home game was just about to start, he decided that he'd really like to see one of those, so once again, as unbelievable as it seemed to me when he told me about it, he wangled a free parking spot somehow, somewhere, and walked over to the stadium.

Of course the game was sold out, but scalpers were everywhere, though he didn't know about that phenome-non and thus didn't know how to approach them. When he observed a man and his daughter in the process of procuring tickets for themselves, he asked them if they could get one for him, too. This they did, and he accom-panied them to their seats. Throughout the game they served as his guides, explaining some of the fine points of NFL football to him.

There you have it: half a dozen different people reached out to be down-home, country friendly to this young man in an environment where I had earlier averred that one is not likely to encounter such behavior. I stand corrected—sort of. I know that his heavy foreign accent and his engaging smile opened doors for him, but I also know that my equally engaging smile would likely have gotten me no more from the guy at the fire station than a "Mister, if you want to park your car, go to a parking lot," followed by underbreath muttering of: "Who does that senile old coot think he is!"

I know, too, that my German friend's naivete could have gotten him into trouble, or maybe even cost him his life, as witness what we've all been reading about big-city violence. But I sometimes wonder if perhaps our paranoid fear of places like downtown Chicago and Detroit turn out to be self-fulfilling prophecies.

Maybe if we just hung a little looser and traveled about in a more relaxed way, we could have more fun in them, and at the same time give the folks who live and work there a chance to prove that friendliness is where you find it—and that one of those places can be downtown Chicago!

# Some Christmas Gift Advice

෨

I have some words of what I hope is wisdom for folks who choose the Christmas season to try to do something about those husbands, sons, fathers, or brothers whom they're so sick of seeing in a particular item of clothing that they're about to buy its replacement and give it to said relatives for Christmas, hoping that when they do the old will be discarded in favor of the new without a backward look. That advice: forget it; you'll be wasting your time.

Perceptive readers have already noticed that the familial designations listed above apply exclusively to the males of our species. There's good reason for that: as far as I've been able to observe, only males develop such a deep affection for a particular cap, coat, sweater, suit, jacket, or tie that they will wear it almost to the exclusion of all others until it or they fall apart at the seams.

Women rarely form such attachments, because they wouldn't think of wearing the same dress to a Christmas party that they had donned for a Thanksgiving social event a few weeks earlier, nor is durability high on their list of criteria when they buy clothing for themselves.

With guys it's different. In 1968 I bought a shirt made out of some kind of blended fabric that was almost literally indestructible but most accommodating in its willingness to reshape itself to every aspect of my body that it covered, from navel, to elbow, to shoulder blades. I stopped wearing it a couple of years ago, but only because one day it mysteriously disappeared from my closet. I should have been forewarned about that event because Judith kept moving it farther and farther back on the clothing bar until finally it wound up right by the wall, squeezed in behind the dining room table extensions that we keep stored there.

I still have moments of depression when I think of that shirt, but after a brief period of mourning for it, I selected another as its replacement, which, I'm sad to say, is beginning its journey down the clothing bar to eventual oblivion.

Lest this piece develop too sad a tone, let me share a happier anecdote with you. My father wore a particular winter cap for upwards of a decade. Because winter caps, with their wool fabric, earflaps, and lining are not as amenable to washing as most other garments, this one developed, over the years, a patina that essentially hid its original color and fabric texture. But my father's love for it increased directly in proportion to my mother's distaste. We all tried to help my mother out on this one because, frankly, we hated that cap as much as she, so we went the Christmas gift route in trying to get him to shed it forever. Dresser drawers at the home place are filled with our failures.

Finally it, too, disappeared. My father, unwilling to risk the break-up of a marriage after sixty-seven years, did not come right out and accuse my mother of flinging it into

the wood furnace in their basement, but he hinted as much to me just before beginning a eulogy for that cap, which began with a story about how it came into his possession and ended with a listing of its many virtues, none of which he ever hoped to find in any other head coverings presently owned or likely to be available on the market today—after which he lapsed into a mood of despondency that I had seen in him only once before, when Franklin Roosevelt dumped his favorite politician, Henry A. Wallace, as his vice-presidential running mate in 1942.

But yesterday, when I stopped by to see my folks, there was a spring to his step and a twinkle in his eye as he took me down into the basement to show me what he had just discovered there. No, it was not that old green cap, which had undoubtedly found its way into the furnace, but another one, which had been much revered before the green one came along, but which my mother had been indiscreet enough to simply hide rather than destroy.

If you insist upon the course of action that I've just warned you against, ask yourself if you can live with the prospect of the garment you selected becoming a favorite, too, and if, in that eventuality, you have the courage that my mother had to do what needs to be done. If the answer is no on both counts, just get him a box of candy and then help him eat it. I don't think you can go wrong with that gift.

# Ethnic Humor: Enough Already!

～

S ome of my best friends tell ethnic jokes, but they're good friends in spite of doing so, not because of it. I am becoming increasingly uncomfortable with that type of humor even though I occasionally laugh at it and, I must confess, have employed it myself a few times. But not recently, nor will I ever again, because in the final analysis it is demeaning to the particular ethnic group that is the butt of it, no matter how vehemently both tellers and listeners proclaim that "it's all in good fun."

I have heard only two ethnic groups used in these jokes here in the Upper Peninsula---Polish people and Finns--- though way back when, I recall a couple told about "dumb Swedes," the adjective in that term mitigating the situation somewhat because it implied the possibility of smart Swedes, a loophole not usually offered the other two groups.

About fifteen years ago the poker club I belong to was made up totally of one ethnic group: Slovenians (we've had ethnic integration in a big way since then). One night a member showed us a sheet of paper with twenty one-liners about Finns, the ethnic group of choice for such jokes around here. Everyone guffawed at the jokes, one of which stated that a Finn's idea of the rhythm method of birth control is to tap his feet on the footboard of the bed while making love. The rest were of like quality and taste.

Because I was still teaching at the time and had the easiest access to a copier, I was assigned the job of reproducing those gems so that others could enjoy them, too. This I did, but wherever the word "Finn" appeared in the originals, I substituted "Slovenian," then handed out the copies at our next poker session. Nobody objected openly to this, but there was a considerable amount of squirming and embarrassed grinning in evidence. As far as I know, not one of my poker buddies ever showed his copy to anyone else.

And I know why: while they read my revised version they momentarily stopped being the other guy—and they didn't like it. We Slovenians are justly proud of our ethnic heritage, as are Finns and Poles, and even though we may smile outwardly when it is the butt of a joke—and maybe even tell a story or two on our own ethnic group—deep down we feel sullied by such humor.

Let me try this one on any fellow Slovenians who might be reading this: How many Slovenians does it take to change a light bulb? Three: one to hold the light bulb and the other two to turn the ladder. Did you feel an unpleasant twinge or two reading this? I did in writing it, even though there is no term comparable to "Polack" that I could use for added effect.

Ethnic jokes are an outgrowth of "moron" jokes, which were discontinued because they ridiculed a group of people who are ill-equipped to defend themselves against them. Now I think it's time to take the next step. I don't suggest eliminating that type of humor totally, because much of what we consider funny depends upon the ineptitude of an individual or group. I still smile when I think of the foreman of a landscaping firm shouting "green side up!" to a group of his workmen laying sod. But I don't want them to be Slovenian workmen, and I don't think my Finnish friends want them to be "Finlanders," or my Polish friends, "Polacks."

Why not use a made-up name for this group in our jokes, one that encompasses the ethnic spectrum and yet represents no group in the real world. My candidate: "Fishgar," an acronym I created from the first letters of several common ethnic groups: French, Italian, Swedish, Hungarian, German, Armenian, and Russian.

The word is not very euphonious, but easy to pronounce and spell, somewhat ridiculous, and, as far as I know, not included in any dictionary of the English language. You could make up one of your own, I suppose, but agreeing upon one makes things simpler. That way, as soon as you hear someone say: "Did you hear about the Fishgar who..." you'll know a joke is coming down the pike and not a true story.

Every word has to begin somewhere, so here goes: A Fishgar read in the newspaper that most accidents happen within ten miles of home—so he moved! All right, so it's not that funny, but it's a start. You take it from there. One suggestion: if you don't consider yourself a member of any ethnic group, try substituting "Yooper" or "American" for the group in the next ethnic joke you're inspired to tell. If you squirm a bit, then perhaps you'll realize that "Fishgar" isn't such a bad idea.

I THOUGHT YOU'D NEVER ASK!

## Music Keeps Drawing Me Back
## to My Roots

∽

This summer I will return for the eighth time in the past twenty five years to Slovenia, the land of my parents' birth and my primary destination on all but one of my trips to Europe. I suppose the fact that Traunik, my home base for most of my sixty-seven years, was so much of an ethnic community during the years of my growing up helped me remain intimately connected with that country.

At the local store I heard Slovenian spoken more often than English, and when I pulled our mail out of Box 43 at the postoffice located in a corner of that store, I frequently found a letter from one of my father's four sisters who remained in the "old country." One of those letters contained the sad news that my father's brother Ivan had been executed at the end of World War II by the Tito government.

During my pre-school days I was as fluent in the Slovenian language as I was in English, and I remember being surprised when I started kindergarten (it was called "chart class" then) by the inability of some of my classmates to understand me when I spoke it.

But I think it was Slovenian music that bound me the most tightly to those overseas roots. There was never a social event at the Traunik hall that didn't feature an impromptu choral group gathered outside its entrance to fill the night air with hauntingly sad or deliciously bawdy ballads that every red-blooded Slovenian-American knew the words to. And when that group moved down into the basement of the hall to lubricate its collective vocal cords with the "pivo" (beer) always available there, the music continued—even more impressive in that confined space.

I was reminded of that scene from my youth just a few weeks ago when I attended an event commemorating the bi-centennial of Bishop Baraga's birth, which was held at St. Peter's Cathedral in Marquette. After the Slovenian-language mass there a reception was held for participants in its basement. It was a stiflingly hot evening, and after washing down a brownie or two with a glass of punch, I started to make my way to the exit for some fresh air.

But I was stopped in my tracks by the same kind of singing that I remembered from my youth. I couldn't believe it! The temperature inside that room was by then almost sauna-like, but at least thirty folks had formed a singing circle and began a performance which mesmerized everyone there. Sweat was by this time literally pouring off their faces, but it mattered not a bit: their music had them in its thrall.

Are Slovenian-Americans maintaining a tradition no longer observed back in the old country? Not at all. On my last trip there I was invited to dinner by relatives from Grosuplje, who hosted us (my cousins Louis and Dick Bartol were my travel companions) in a little country inn outside that city. Small establishments like that one are much more common in Europe than in the United States.

The room we were in held only the sixteen of us and another couple, who obligingly left early on so that the event could be totally a family affair. We brought with us a typically American attitude toward public dining places: "eat and run." But after doing the eating part we knew such would not be the case that evening.

Our waiter brought in four bottles of a good Slovenian wine, and our host and his family pushed away from the table far enough to be comfortable but close enough to reach that wine, after which began a serenade that was to last an hour and a half. Our host was a member of a singing group, and it seemed that every member of his family was equally musically inclined.

What differentiated this singing from the "Dirty Lil, dirty Lil, lived on top of garbage hill..." kind that I have sometimes participated in stateside was its professionalism. Each singer knew his part, and before some of the more complex numbers, they would get together for a moment, like football players in a huddle, and then come out singing. And what singing it was! Our host's daughter-in-law was a student of music and literature at the University of Ljubljana at the time, and when she and her husband sang a love duet, I can honestly say that no operatic aria has ever sounded better to me.

Just before it was time to go home, our Slovenian relatives looked over at Dick, Louis, and me and said it was now our turn to do the singing and theirs to do the listening. They requested, if you can believe it, our Star-Spangled Banner. Our own vocal cords somewhat lubricated by the red wine, we stood up and offered a rendition that warranted an invitation from the Green Bay Packers to do the same at Lambeau Field.

I know that for me it was the first time I was able to sing the last lines of our national anthem without switching keys!

Several days later, our visits with relatives behind us, we did the tourist thing, stopping in Bled, Slovenia's most popular tourist attraction. There we encountered a young American school teacher, who was attracted to us, not by our good looks, but by the fact that she overheard us speaking English. We learned that she had accepted employment as a music teacher in a high school over there, and when we asked her when she was planning to return to the U.S., she said: "I'd like to go back to teach music in the States, but I can't. Kids over here love music. They hang on my every word. That's just not the way it is back home."

I don't know whether or not she was totally right about that, but I do know that I'll be sojourning in Bled for three days on this trip. Perhaps I'll run into her again so that I'll be able to ask her if she still feels that way. One thing for sure: music will be an important part of my day there, as I hope it is of yours, wherever you may be.

# A Bowling Comeback—Sort Of

∾

**M**ost sporting activities are considerably more difficult to get good at than the typical armchair quarterback or other observer of them tends to realize. This truth was brought home to me a couple of months ago when a good friend finally persuaded me to try my hand at bowling again, a pastime that I had last engaged in over thirty years ago.

I've watched that sport on television from time to time in recent years and have concluded that there isn't really a whole lot to it: one just rolls a ball in the general direction of ten pins, which will obligingly fall down as long as that ball makes some sort of contact with the lone pin in the front row.

Certainly a guy like me, with a powerful left arm that can still propel a sixteen-pound ball down the alley with about the same rhythm and speed employed thirty years ago, should be able to hold his own with the best of them. Of course, over those years I have managed to completely obliterate the memory of my singular lack of talent in that arena, which is what caused me to quit in the first place.

So I showed up at the Eastwood Lanes in Marquette just before Christmas with a bowling ball and a pair of old high-topped bowling shoes that I had resurrected from the chicken coop on the home place, where I had retired them in frustration and failure in the early sixties.

The "old pros," who vaguely remembered equipment which looked like that but had abandoned it long ago, were kind enough just to smile at the spectacle, reserving their snickers and good-natured ridicule for later sessions when I would become one of the guys and thus a legitimate target for such rituals.

Dame Fortune has a sense of humor, a wicked one, in case you haven't noticed, and at the end of the fifth frame of my first game my score was 110. It seemed that pins were falling down in anticipation of the arrival of that old, black, much-nicked hunk of ebonite heading for them. By extrapolation I reasoned that at the end of the game I'd have a score of at least 220, which would put me right up with the guys on TV and would validate my judgment as to the simplicity and ease of bowling.

But then Fortune kicked the pins out from under me, in a manner of speaking, by leaving several of them standing after I had thrown the requisite two balls at them in the remaining frames. My score at the end of the first game: 177. Some slight doubt crept over me as I proceeded to game two, in which I scored a 151, and true perplexity took over as I finished with a 119.

I have returned to the Eastwood Lanes just about every Monday afternoon since then, trying to remember what I had done in those first five frames of game one that I was no longer doing. But deep down I knew the truth: those early frames had been pure luck, and it takes talent and practice to get good at bowling, just as it does at skiing, golf, tennis, or any other game you care to name. But I also learned something else: you don't have to be good to have fun—something I didn't understand when I quit bowling three decades ago.

Bowling is a game of comradeship the way we play it on Monday afternoons at Eastwood. There are no team standings (because there are no teams), and averages aren't kept, so each session marks a new beginning. Every bowler genuinely roots for every other one, and each strike or difficult spare conversion generates a high-five, or rather a low-five, accomplished by the gentle tapping of the for-the-moment successful bowler's hand as he walks back to his seat to bask in the glory of his accomplishment. I was the recipient of a couple of those low-fives last week, one coming when I converted a 4-7-10 split—pure luck again, but I basked anyway.

There is as much diversity in bowling styles as there is in the shape, size, and age of the participants, and because one spends no more than a quarter of his time at the alley actually throwing balls at pins, there's plenty available for observation and analysis of other bowlers, with some left for conversation.

Six sessions into my resumed bowling "career," I'm now fairly certain that I'll never be any more of a success at it than I was the first time around, but I'm glad Ken Johnson talked me into coming back to it. I like the camaraderie, and I don't even mind the comments about my battered old bowling ball, which I have not yet been willing to exchange for a new reactive resin or urethane ball like the ones my fellow bowlers are rolling.

I did abandon those old high-topped leather shoes which saw me through so much mediocre bowling way back when in favor of a brightly-colored, modish new pair. But I'm going back to them next session. Those new ones just don't feel right. Old ball, old shoes, and a getting-older bowler—if there's a good game somewhere in my future,

I want us to do it as a threesome, for old time's sake.

Now that I know one can go back again to enjoy a long-abandoned activity, there are a couple of others I think I'll give a try. I go by the Marquette Mountain Ski Area quite often, and I remember that my old skis are stored right next to where I had kept my bowling ball. Why not!

# It's Time to Unmask the Dreaded Asterisk

❧

During my thirty-one years of English teaching I worked with upwards of three thousand students, and I want to apologize to any of them reading this essay for my failure to teach them about the dreaded asterisk. I was so caught up in doing things like writing the sentence, "When are we going to eat, Mother?" on the chalkboard and then erasing the comma to show how important punctuation can be to meaning that I never got around to warning them that the presence of an asterisk can have life-or-death implications for them, just as the comma does for the mother in the sample sentence.

Most teachers, from kindergarten on, share this failure. We should never have been saying: "A is for apple..." but rather: "A Is for asterisk so starlike and cold. Heed not its warnings and miseries unfold," when teaching the alphabet to those kindergartners, thereby laying the groundwork for intensive instruction on that important punctuation mark later.

I've reached this conclusion because I have been

encountering the asterisk more and more lately. It is a somewhat unobtrusive little mark, which I probably ignored as often as I noticed until I made it a point to be on the alert for it (MY teachers failed me in that department, too!)

If I were in charge of things, I would require a warning, such as there presently is on cigaret packages, on any printed material containing asterisks. Suggested wording: "WARNING: the following page contains one or more asterisks. Research has shown that failure to read the material these marks call attention to can be hazardous to your health—or finances."

The asterisk is so common today because of various disclosure regulations to consumers which can be met as long as certain information about a product is divulged, no matter how small it is printed or in how inconspicuous a location it appears. I have so far looked in vain for a car lease advertisement that says IN LARGE PRINT: "After you make a down payment of $3,000 you will pay $299 a month to drive our Infracta Supra for four years, at the end of which time you will return the car to us and we'll keep all the money you paid us."

The large print in the ad will extol the virtues of a particular car and the wisdom of your leasing it. But there will be an asterisk somewhere in that copy, which will direct you to some words written at the end of the ad in such fine print that you will need a magnifying glass to read them.

In the world of commerce, asterisked material is almost always used to reveal information that the advertiser would prefer that the we not attend to. Thus we read about the amazing qualities of a particular pain killer in large, sometimes bold-faced, print and then are directed by an asterisk to a list of about twenty conditions under which that medication must not be used, sometimes written in print so small that even a magnifying glass won't help.

Maybe an even better idea than warning labels for asterisked material would be a law forbidding them entirely in the world of business so that everything would be "up front" and obvious, and the true annual interest rate on a credit purchase, for instance, would appear in print at least as large as that used to brag about the product being sold. And wouldn't it be nice to read something like the following: "This is a great bathroom cleaning product, but if you try to use it on acrylic finishes, you can do some pretty serious damage." I must tell you that I'm not holding my breath until such things happen.

If I were back in the classroom today, I would teach my students to be good asterisk scanners, and I would get them in the habit of reading asterisked material a couple of times before even beginning to peruse the rest of the text. This could same them considerable time—and money. I might even ask them to estimate how much of the latter they saved in a particular situation and send a small portion of it to me as a token of their gratitude.*

And remember, kindergarten teachers, next fall: "A is for asterisk so starlike and cold. Heed not its warnings and miseries unfold."

* Readers should interpret the preceding statement as an attempt by the writer to introduce some levity into an otherwise-serious subject. In no way does it imply that teachers should EVER accept gifts of money from their students.

# You've Come a Long Way, Baby, but Did You Have to Drive So Fast?

൚

"Y ou've come a long way, Baby" said a cigarette commercial of the 70's about the American woman of that period. Indeed Baby HAS come a long way, and nowadays just about every time I step into my automobile I'm made aware of just how Baby has managed to come so far so fast: she has found the accelerator of her automobile—with a vengeance!

A couple of decades ago, whenever I closed in on a slow-moving car ahead of me, I could quite accurately conclude that it was a woman driver or an elderly man. The elderly man part still holds (with some exceptions, of course), but I haven't been overtaking and passing many women drivers lately. On the contrary, they have been passing ME with depressing regularity, even though I've been issued enough speeding tickets over the years to demonstrate that I'm not exactly a slow driver myself.

I'm having a bit of trouble with that, maybe because when I got my first driver's license at the end of World War II, women drivers, slow or fast, were the exception rather than the rule. Young ladies then depended on their knight in shining chromium to drive them where they wanted to go—or in many cases where he wanted to take them—and older ladies sat staidly alongside their husbands on the front passenger seat.

All that began to change after the war, when Rosie the Riveter and the many other young women who played such an important role in our winning it decided that they didn't want to play the automobile game by those rules any more. Lest I be labeled a male chauvinist, I think I supported that change at the time and, looking back, I certainly do now.

But having watched my older sister tear off a garage door jamb and part of the bumper of a '36 Chevrolet during a mostly futile driver's training lesson from my father while she was still a high school student, I've never totally rid myself of the notion that driving is just not quite as natural a process for the female of our species as it is for the male.

Neither was I able, until all those women drivers started passing me, to rid myself of the notion that every woman driver was beautiful—and exciting, because it seemed to me back in the forties that my few female contemporaries who had gotten the hang of driving and were doing a substantial amount of it had those qualities.

Many probably didn't, but during that split second when our cars were side by side as we met on the highway I was able to create in my imagination ravishingly beautiful creatures whom I knew I would have fallen in love with if we weren't ships, or rather cars, meeting in the night.

Now that they've started passing me, though, I've been able to scrutinize them more closely, and I've come to find out that most are plain garden variety folks, just like us guys, and they're hurrying to and from the same places we are in this equal opportunity world.

They tend to be young, though, these female speeders. And they seem to favor smaller cars. It's a bit of a shock to see a Geo Metro go whizzing by, a young lady sitting as casually behind the wheel as she would if she were home in an easy chair. I find that scary, just as I do her disinclination to pay the slightest attention to anything or anyone around her.

Women drivers, fast or slow, just don't check things out around them as much as guys when they drive, or at least they don't seem to. One day a couple of years ago Judith and I left Escanaba together, she behind in our car and I up ahead in the pickup, which was loaded with cedar paneling.

About a mile south of Rapid River my pickup motor died suddenly, and as I coasted to a stop on the shoulder of the highway I was relieved when I looked in the rear view mirror to see Judith's car approaching. I shouldn't have been! Without so much as a glance in my direction she shot by me and drove the remaining twenty-seven miles home, leaving me no choice but to hitch a ride to Rapid River for help——I'll spare you the rest of the details of that misadventure.

Yes, I know: women must be paying attention to the things that count because they still have fewer serious accidents than men, but I understand that they're rapidly achieving parity in that department, too, and will probably soon pass them——at least if they keep passing me on the highway the way they've been doing.

I got my inspiration for this piece yesterday, when a platinum-blonde, middle-aged, anxious-to-get-somewhere woman shot past me as I was driving to Marquette. Her left hand held a telephone into which she was speaking intently, and with her right I'm reasonably sure that she was sorting some papers on the seat beside her. I'll give her the benefit of the doubt on that last observation, however, because that would leave her no hands to steer with. Now that IS a scary thought!

# Reading Should Not Be a Contest

∞

This morning I saw in our local daily newspaper photographs of two Michigan educators, one of whom was being fed a couple of live night crawlers and the other of whom was about to have her head sheared. Both of these indignities were being tolerated by these folks because they said they would submit to them if students in their schools read a total of x number of books within a certain period.

I suppose I will be considered a spoil sport for saying this, but I was not amused, though I have no doubt that the kids were and that those educators were perceived by them to have qualities of humanness and sportsmanship absent from many of their kind. And I don't question anyone's motives here nor the likelihood that more books or pages of books were read, or at least glanced at or lied about, than would have been the case in the absence of this gimmicky contest.

But I'm not happy with the message this activity sent to young readers: that reading itself may not be much fun, but if doing it can get old Mr. So and So to eat a live worm or two, we might as well give it a try. At this juncture I can see the lightbulb over the heads of folks who have already decided to disagree with me as they say: "Aha! You've just made our point: the end justifies the means. Anything goes when it comes to getting Johnnie or Janie to read."

Well, maybe, but having taught English for thirty-one years and having employed a gimmick or two myself in my attempts to nurture a love for reading in my students, I know now that those gimmicks just didn't do the trick. Rewards work best when they motivate someone to do something unpleasant or at least unenjoyable. If Johnnie is given an extra dollar's allowance for every week he takes the garbage out without being reminded to do so, he may well get into the habit, but he will never get to the point where he enjoys taking out the garbage—and God forbid that he should.

And Janie may be willing to read some extra pages again next year for the pleasure of seeing someone shear her teacher once more, but I doubt that she'll like reading one bit better than she did before she engaged in one of these "contests. I'm afraid all they do is put emphasis upon having read, when it really belongs on reading—and, more important, the enjoyment of reading.

We're into numbers these days, and speed. I've recently been listening, to the point of wanting to throw up, to a radio commercial promising that we all can be taught to read a 500-page book in two hours with almost total recall of its contents. I don't know whether I feel sorrier for the person who thinks that can be done or the one who thinks it's a good idea.

Maybe I'm feeling this way right now because I just completed reading a book with more enjoyment than I derived from any such activity since those halcyon days of my growing up when Zane Grey and James Oliver

Curwood were my authors of choice. Back then I didn't read a book; rather, I entered into it on page one and emerged from it at the other end with a feeling of regret that I was at the "having read" stage of the process.

That happened to me again just last week with the re-reading, after fifty-five years, of Marjorie Kinnan Rawlings' masterpiece, *The Yearling*. I confess that I, too, have been guilty in recent years of being anxious to get to the end of any novel I began, and the only reason I didn't bring that attitude to this one is that I was reading it in a very special way.

I had bought the book in Slovenia on my last trip over there with the idea of reading it back home to broaden my knowledge of the Slovenian language, and now that I'm returning for another visit I was motivated to finally do so. First I read a chapter in the English version, carefully and with attention to every word in it. Speed wasn't important to me, but understanding was, because that would help me decipher each sentence in Slovenian.

It took me more than a week of reading, a couple of hours each evening, to complete the book, and I put it down sadly, not only because it has a sad ending but because I didn't want to leave Penny, Ora, and Jody Baxter. And I had developed some affection, or at least sympathy, for those Forrester boys, who lived down the road a piece from the Baxters—even Lem, who did some very nasty things. The Florida scrub country that was the setting for *The Yearling* was described so vividly by the author that I have no need to go to it to experience it.

When I was about twelve, the same age as Jody in the novel, I had to shoot my pet cat because our hay mowing machine had cut off all four of its legs as it hunted mice in the field.

So when Jody had to destroy his pet deer because it had been ruining every crop the Baxters tried to raise, I understood in a very special way what he went through. And I'm not ashamed to admit that when I came to that climactic moment in the book, I cried as hard as I ever remember doing in connection with a story at the loss of innocence and the important move toward growing up that this act represented.

Of course I wouldn't have responded this way if Marjorie Kinnan Rawlings weren't such a talented writer. I hope those kids who participated in the reading events I began this piece with read good books—there's a lot of junk being written these days—and weren't too consumed by numbers to enjoy and understand them.

If someone could come up with a machine that measured enjoyment and understanding, and a group of students reached a pre-set goal in those, I just might be willing, if I were still teaching, to have my head sheared. As for worm eating, Judith thinks that blood sausage and a couple of other ethnic delicacies that I eat with such relish would make that less than a giant leap for me.

# Automotive Gadgets—Why Can't We Resist Them?

∾

What a difference a day makes! Until yesterday my new-car plans were pretty well set: wait until spring and then order a new Chevrolet Lumina to replace the 1990 model whose odometer is about to turn 70,000. I used to wait until I had driven a car 90-100,000 miles before I got new-car fever, but my son Mark's employment at GM entitles me to a fairly hefty discount on a GM vehicle once a year, so I now have no problem rationalizing my way to more frequent changes.

Besides, this new Lumina has been substantially changed from the one I'm now driving, with such things as anti-lock brakes, airbags for driver and front-seat passenger, and a few bells and whistles that car designers hadn't dreamed up yet back in 1990. I was convinced that there isn't a whole lot more that anybody could possibly want on his next car than what will be available on this one—until yesterday morning, when I read that there will be a car in the market in this country in 1996 that will offer as one of its options a refrigerated glove compartment.

Now I must tell you that until I read about this in the automotive section of my newspaper, I hadn't spent a whole lot of time thinking to myself that a refrigerated glove compartment would really improve my life. In recent years I've been having more and more trouble even finding the glove compartment, and I don't remember the last time I put anything into it.

But apparently some folks have been depositing such things as chocolate candy in theirs, which has been melting into a gooey mass, and doubtless thousands of auto owners have been writing to the Big Three to tell them that something has to be done about this problem. I confess that I have such a passion for chocolate that none in my possession has ever lasted long enough to be stored in the glove compartment of my car even if I were ever able to find it.

Anyway, it is now virtually inevitable that by the year 2,000 no car will be built without a refrigerated glove compartment, because automobile manufacturers have taken the concept of "monkey see, monkey do" to new heights, or should I say "depths." And all those folks who make their living writing about new cars have helped the process along by downgrading a particular vehicle because it doesn't contain a feature that another in its class has.

But we, the consumers, are most at fault because, no matter how we protest to the contrary, we have so far bought into just about any automotive gimmick that has come down the pike at us. Some cars now have automatic dual-controlled heating and air-conditioning systems which permit the driver to select an in-car climate different from the one which his front-seat passenger prefers. And there are now computerized seat controls which adjust automatically to as many as four drivers with the push of a button.

A few weeks ago I rode in a car that was able to recognize its owner (or whoever had the remote locking control in his possession) from fifty feet away, unlocking itself as he approached and locking itself if he was moving away from it. The list goes on, but I won't. Of course, some features, but certainly not the majority, actually DO improve the convenience and/or the safety of a car. We just ought to get better at determining what they are and say no to the rest.

Alas, the the validity of the old adage: "Don't cry, little luxury, don't cry: you'll be a necessity by and by!" is being demonstrated more and more frequently in the automobile world these days by consumers who just can't resist all that gimmickry. I once thought that being able to open the trunk of my car by pushing a button under the dash was gimmickry, but it came with my last car, which I bought "off the lot," so I put up with it. It stopped functioning a couple of months ago, and I'm embarrassed to confess that I've been having a tough time dealing with that "old-fashioned" system of having to go outside to open the trunk with my key.

I'm going to try to exercise some common sense when I sit across from Al Peterson in a couple of months over at Frei's to place my order, but I'll probably "what the heck, why not" myself into a couple of thousand dollars worth of options that will take me far past the basic transportation that I keep telling myself is all I want in a car. At least for the moment, though, I won't have to make a decision on that refrigerated glove compartment.

# Another Digital Defeat

∾

I have never gotten comfortable with things digital, and I have complained several times in my columns about digital watches, car speedometers, and other devices which deal with numbers. That's why I can't understand the presence of a brand-new digital scale in our bathroom, which I recently bought to replace a scale that had expired after a quarter century of faithful service.

It's not that I was without a choice in the matter when I confronted the scale section in a local department store. In fact, I had in my hands for a few moments one of the old-fashioned kind with innards that twirl, compress, and do other things mechanical which cause a dial to go through a few gyrations before settling down and allowing itself to be read.

But, somehow, I walked out with one of the digital kind, and if it doesn't have the decency to break very soon, I guess I'll just have to live with it, because I can't deal with two scales in our house at the same time, and I'm a bit too frugal to discard the new one—just yet.

I THOUGHT YOU'D NEVER ASK!

What's my particular beef? Well, I like to be as actively involved in any operation I'm part of as possible, and a digital scale offers absolutely no opportunity for that. One simply stands on it and waits for it to flash a number, for most of us one that's higher than what we had in mind.

I like the way it used to be with scales. I got my early weigh-ins on one in our basement that my dad had there primarily to weigh butchered chickens before delivering them to market. I had to "operate" that scale if I wanted any results from it. First I selected from a tray of weights the appropriate one for my weight range and hung it on a rod suspended from the end of a beam. Then I slid another weight along that beam until it balanced, after which I read the number closest to the front edge of that sliding weight. Voila! I now knew my weight—and I had been an important part of the process.

It was a delicate business. If I tapped the sliding weight too vigorously, it shot past the balance point and the process had to be repeated in reverse. There was a knack to it. I don't know precisely what a knack is, but people talked a lot more about knacks in those halcyon pre-digital days. They were constantly saying that so and so had a knack for such and such.

My uncle Lud Lustick had one for fixing cars. He could open a hood, listen to what was going on underneath it, and make the necessary adjustments to get the motor purring again. Today's mechanic requires skill more complex than a knack, but not nearly as mystical, as he hooks up a dozen or more instruments to that motor and waits for digital read-outs.

I digress. Scales are what I'm writing about today. The balance beam kind is a little too bulky for our small bathroom and too expensive for our scale budget. But had I opted for the one with the twirling dial, I would have continued to be at least a small part of the action.

For one thing I could have observed the cause and effect relationship between my stepping on the scale and its doing visible things. My old scale always read "0" when I was not on it, and if it didn't I could make adjustments by using a little button on the back of it.

That's another thing I liked about pre-digital instruments. One could make adjustments. I think the opportunity to make adjustments is very important in the maintenance of good mental health, and I'm not comfortable having to take it on faith that our new scale knows what it's doing all by itself. It shows me nothing whatever unless I switch it on with my toe, at which point a zero flashes on the small screen.

But I'd better make up my mind to get on board without any dilly-dallying or it turns itself off again. Dilly-dallying, another great saver of mental health, was a lot easier for folks when digital everythings weren't doing visible countdowns (and sometimes invisible ones) to remind us that time's a'wasting.

Finally, I had an opportunity to affect the read-out on our old scale. In recent years, I've been interested in smaller numbers, so I've been in the habit of weighing myself in the morning before my shower, when I have nothing on but my attitude, and I'd ease myself every so gently onto the scale, watching those numbers roll by as I did so. I developed a knack for that which does me no good whatsoever with our new scale.

O.K., you may reasonably ask: why didn't I think of all that before I walked out of that department store? I have a theory: we can complain about all that electronic technology, but we are doomed by forces beyond our control to succumb to it anyway. Otherwise why did I order out our latest car with "remote keyless entry," which makes it possible for me to lock or unlock its doors when I'm still thirty feet away from it!

# Fame: Even Fifteen Minutes May Be Too Much

∾

T he eighteenth century English poet Thomas Gray, in what I think is one of the really great poems in the English language, "Elegy in a Country Churchyard," tells us that "full many a flower is born to blush unseen and waste its sweetness on the desert air." I first read that poem when I was still in high school, and I was strangely comforted by the idea in that line because, as bashful and retiring as I was in my adolescence, I fully expected to blush unseen for the rest of my life.

It hasn't quite turned out that way. But long after I decided that being bashful and retiring wasn't getting me anywhere, I didn't feel that I was receiving a whole lot more attention than Gray's flower in the desert. Then along came Andy Warhol to promise me that somewhere along the line I could expect at least fifteen minutes of fame.

Now "fame" is a pretty powerful word, even defined as modestly as it must be to give most of us a crack at it. It certainly means more than a pat on the head for a deed well done or, in my case, a question from someone I meet on the street: "Aren't you the guy who writes that column in our paper?" For one thing, the asker all too often seems to imply by his tone that he'd really like me to quit doing it.

Nevertheless, I came within an eyelash of achieving that fifteen minutes a few years ago when the Superior Central Cougars made the final four in the state Class D basketball tournament. That team was made up of players who, up until the year before, had played for the Trenary Comets or the Eben Eagles, and the new team was formed after the schools consolidated.

I wrote a narrative poem about their exploits, which I was asked to recite to a crowd gathered at the school gym to celebrate the team's return from downstate. When I read the last quatrain of that poem, which went as follows:

"Some started out as Eagles,
And some were Comets bright,
But they all turned into Cougars,
And it was an awesome sight!"

that crowd rose to its feet as one in a crescendo of applause and cheers. This was it, I thought, the beginning of my fifteen minutes, and I savored the prospect of mingling with the crowd after the program to receive continued adulation.

But everyone seemed more interested in the refreshments being served or the two television monitors which were replaying the glory moments of the Cougars. I was tempted to start tapping folks on the shoulder and asking: "Remember me? I'm the guy who just read that poem. How did you like it?" But even I am not brazen enough to do that, so I just drove home, comforting myself with the notion that what I had experienced was just a sample. The big moment was still ahead of me.

It came one day a couple of years later, when I was asked to do a book signing at the B. Dalton Bookstore in the Marquette Mall. Its huge advertising sign, easily seen by folks passing by on U.S. 41, featured my name—in lights yet! This time I was taking no chances. I bought a hamburger at a local fast food place and sat in my car for fifteen minutes to eat it, gazing up at that sign between bites.

Then I went inside to await those hordes of people who I was confident would come in to buy my book. The first person to drop by didn't purchase a book but announced that she was writing an article for a newsletter I edit, and she thought that would be a good time to discuss it with me. It was, because, believe it or not, no long line of folks waiting for my autograph had formed.

My next visitor I recognized immediately as a gentleman who had written several letters to the editor chastising me—quite vigorously and scornfully, I might add—for a pro-gun-control position I had taken in several of my columns. He was a formidable-appearing fellow. Just before he began his walk toward the table where I sat, I thought I could see his right arm hanging low and slightly away from his body, ready to reach for a holstered gun at his side.

By the time he had taken his third step, he had been converted by my imagination into Jack Palance, in the movie "Shane," and I was that poor sodbuster about to be blown into the next world by a Colt .45 Instinctively, I shoved back my chair, stood up, and reached for the the only weapon I had at hand, a copy of my book, *A Season of Benign Neglect.* Fortunately I didn't have to use it, because when he came close I could see that he was almost as decent as most people who agree with me, and we had a civil, though not particularly friendly, conversation on the issue that had brought him in to see me.

Lest I paint too bleak a picture of the experience, I want you to know that I DID sell a few books that day, though a line never did form at my table. But when I packed up

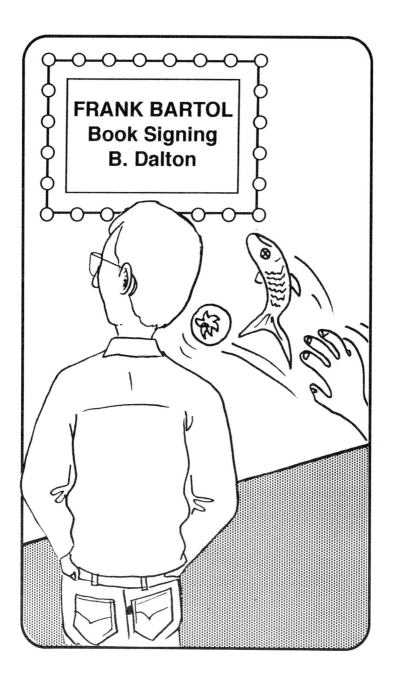

my remaining books and went home, I had a more sophisticated awareness of fame: even in the very small dose that I had just experienced it, is a double-edged sword and maybe one shouldn't wish for it too much.

# You've Got to Accentuate the Positive

∿

I've never doubted that there is something to the power of positive thinking, accentuating the positive, looking on the bright side and all those other notions promoted by the late Norman Vincent Peale, among others. But I don't consciously test them in my own life very often. One day last week, though, when a gray day and a return to colder weather in combination with a schedule overloaded with less-than-pleasant responsibilities put me in a blue funk that I didn't want repeated, I thought I'd give them a try.

I promised myself that when I got up the next morning I would pay special attention to anything pleasant that happened to me and, like that character in Voltaire's "Candide," I'd keep reminding myself that this is "the best of all possible worlds," and that I couldn't be happier. Thus when I confronted my breakfast grapefruit and found it sweet and juicy, I generated the first pleasure vibes that I would try to sustain throughout the day. It's been a so-so year for grapefruit, in my judgment, and I have to admit that it had been my habit to gripe about the ones that made my lips pucker rather than to wax ecstatic about the good ones.

The grapefruit consumed, I went for my toast, both slices of which Judith, quite by accident, had buttered on their wide sides, which meant that they offered the maximum surface possible for me to spread jam on. Though she continues to put breakfast in front of me every morning (a quid pro quo for equally solicitous behavior on my part elsewhere), I have never been able to get her to pay the slightest attention to which side of my toast she butters. I do the bread baking here—one of those quid pro quos— and I prefer round loaves, which generate slices with easily discernible "wide sides."

Sweet grapefruit, properly-buttered toast—it doesn't get much better than that at the breakfast table, I kept saying to myself. And, not wanting to over-do things, I chose to lay off the happiness button for the rest of that meal. But after it, when I went to brush my teeth, I slid open the medicine cabinet door in our bathroom to confront a brand-new tube of toothpaste! There is something almost indecent about the pleasure I get when my right hand encircles a full tube of toothpaste, which yields its contents with the slightest squeeze of my fingers. And that day, when I was on pleasure alert, I consciously intensified that feeling.

Having grown up during the Depression, I'm into frugality enough so that I feel obliged to coax the last blob of toothpaste out of the tube before consigning it to the wastebasket, a chore made more unpleasant than it was in those halcyon pre-plastic days, when a tube once folded stayed that way instead of uncoiling to its full length immediately after use the way plastic does.

Staying on course with my program became a bit tougher when I stepped outside to face the day as I went to the post office to mail about fifty Alger County Historical

Society membership receipts. An overnight freeze followed by a light dusting of snow produced unbelievably slippery concrete steps leading down to our driveway. I negotiated the first four, but the fifth sent me out into space, and in landing I wrenched my right shoulder more than a little, launching those fifty envelopes into the air as I fell.

It took me several minutes to retrieve all of them, four of which, somehow, wound up under my pickup, and one was grabbed by my dog, who thought it was a good time for a game of "keep away." But I chose to be grateful for the opportunity to double-check those envelopes as I reassembled them into a bundle to make sure a stamp was affixed to each one, and it occurred to me that a wrenched right shoulder was no big deal for a left-handed guy.

I back-slid rather dramatically after that, I must admit, at least partly out of concern that I might be picked up by those men in white suits if I continued to smile my way about in a world where a lot of bad things were happening everywhere.

But that brief experiment did show me that there is value in looking on the bright side, and that most of us can find something to be happy about on any given day if we but concentrate on doing so.

I THOUGHT YOU'D NEVER ASK!

# Golden Wedding Anniversaries:
# An Endangered Ritual

∾

I read in the newspaper the other day about a couple from Eben Junction, Walter and Helen Maki, who had just celebrated their golden wedding anniversary. I was a bit surprised by this news because it wasn't so long ago that I had watched them schussbooming down the Slapneck ski hill and doing various other things that I tend to connect more with youth than the age they had to have reached to be married fifty years. Just about every contact I've made with them in recent years has reinforced the image of two people in the prime of life, who enjoy being with each other and plan to grow old together—when they get around to it.

I sat next to the male half of that couple at a basketball game last week and tried to extract from him some formula for a successful long marriage that I could pass on to my readers. But most folks around here know that I'm in the writing business--sort of—these days and are somewhat skittish about sharing too much with me for fear of being featured in one of my essays.

So I had to settle for several vague generalizations on the subject, which I will strive to flesh out with observations from my own marital experience. After all, Judith and I just celebrated our fortieth anniversary this past August, which I think qualifies me as somewhat of an expert on the subject of matrimony.

We are now in what should be the golden age of golden wedding anniversaries. When I was growing up, the Biblical "three score and ten" for one's life span was about as much as a person could hope for, so folks didn't live long enough to celebrate a half century of marital bliss very often. We had only one such celebration that I can remember in the Traunik Hall before World War II, which was treated like a monumental event indeed.

We had only one divorce, too, which was viewed as an even more monumental event. We didn't celebrate it at the hall, of course, but we might as well have done so for all the attention it got in the community. Today, if you were to ask the old-timers around here (my God, I'm one of them!) the name of that divorced lady, they would lay it on you without a moment's hesitation, but ask the younger generation to list the divorced folks they know, they'd be at a loss to do so, because being divorced is too common a status to get any of their attention at all.

So there you have it: we now live long enough to make golden wedding celebrations a distinct possibility for most married couples—but we don't love long enough. And we don't tolerate enough, and we don't adapt enough, and we don't do enough of a good many other things that would help make today's marriages last.

What we do too much of is pattern our married lives after what we see of marriage in soap operas and read of it in pulp romance novels, which are by far the most popular printed material these days. I have to admit that I read and enjoyed *The Bridges of Madison County*, but looking back on it now I acknowledge that what it was saying basically was that marital love is pretty humdrum stuff. Husbands go to state fairs with their kids so that really exciting love can find its way to wives in their absence via a battered old pickup truck driven by a bronzed, tough, good looking dude who was poured into jeans he is fully prepared to remove so that he can demonstrate his marathon lovemaking talents.

The stereotypical wife in much of pulp romance fiction (forget Francesca for a moment) is so preoccupied with taking care of the kids and trying to pick out just the right wallpaper for the bedroom that she doesn't tend to other bedroom things, which makes it okay for her husband to search out a woman who "understands" him and is prepared to fulfill his fantasy of the moment.

Those of us who took the "till death do us part" words of the wedding ceremony seriously are getting to be an endangered species, rowing our matrimonial boats upstream against an increasingly faster current, which threatens to swamp the institution of marriage itself.

So hats off to my friends in Eben and all those others who celebrated their fiftieth anniversary this year or are about to, as well as to those many middle-aged couples like Judith and me (old age is a state of mind, I keep telling myself) who have no intention of turning our boats around or scuttling them.

Please don't write to tell me that staying married is not always a good idea. I know that very well. But I know it's a good one much more often than not, and if it weren't for a long held skepticism about formulas and recipes for any successful social institutions, I'd offer a couple in closing. That and the realization that Judith and I still have a decade to go before we can be members of the golden anniversary club prompt me to say simply: "Go thou and do likewise," and let it go at that.

# A Cold-Weather Spectator? Not Me!

∾

I didn't participate in any way in the U.P. 200 sled dog race last weekend, though I was tempted for a moment to drive over to Chatham, only nine miles from my home, to watch the beginning of the midnight run and to cheer on the mushers who started from Marquette as they hit this check point in the big race.

But memories of earlier cold-weather spectator activities kept me glued to my Lazyboy watching and listening to a reporter on local television interview folks of all ages who HAD braved the cold—who, as a matter of fact, looked as if they weren't braving anything at all but just enjoying themselves. I didn't pay much attention to what they were saying, because I was preoccupied with their ruddy cheeks, their effervescent smiles, and the warmth that seemed to emanate from their bodies. And I thought for a moment about what television viewers would have seen and heard had I been one of those spectators interviewed.

It was a sobering thought, but one which made me glad I had stayed put in a warm place. You see, I have a circulatory system that keeps me so warm when I go cross-country skiing, even in very cold weather, that after a few minutes I will often remove my gloves. But that same system completely ignores my body's need for warmth when I am not active.

Fifteen minutes of sitting in the stands on a cold November evening watching a football game, or perched at the bottom of Suicide Hill watching ski jumpers, or (my most recent winter spectator activity) standing on Northern Michigan University's snow-covered football field watching my son Dan compete in snowshoe races during the Special Olympics winter games turns me almost literally into an icicle.

But icicles look good, their color natural for them, whereas my cheeks, nose, and chin, the only parts of my anatomy left uncovered in these situations, assume most of the various shades of purple which are given a name. It is not a pretty sight! And to make matters worse, my muscular and skeletal systems shift into a state of semi-paralysis, so I lurch about in my attempts to keep warm in a way which would prompt onlookers to conclude that I had been doing some elbow bending with Jack Daniels.

That impression would be strengthened if those same onlookers engaged me in conversation out there. I am generally pleased with my voice, and thirty-one years of teaching English and speech have helped me to speak my native language reasonably "trippingly on the tongue." But when a lovely young lady from NMU, who was out there on that same frozen expanse with other co-eds, cheering those Special Olympic performers on, came bouncing up to me to make some friendly comments as I knelt in the snow adjusting the bindings on Dan's snowshoes, all I could come up with by way of repartee was: "Angh gertz wwig cooln..." She bounced away as briskly as she had come, and I considered running after her to tell her how much better I talk when my vocal apparatus isn't frozen.

I didn't, of course. But I thought about an earlier time when lovely young ladies were a more important part of my life. Back in 1950 I invited the then love of my life, who was attending neighboring Carroll College, to the homecoming football game between Marquette University (where I was a student) and Holy Cross.

Ours had been a warm-weather romance, begun in June, but that November day in Milwaukee was bitter cold, and this charming co-ed, whose own cold-weather thermostat was working quite well, probably didn't think very highly of the purple, shivering mass of humanity at her side, whom even several hours in a Milwaukee nightclub after the game couldn't warm up to a usable state. She was kind enough not to say anything, but we broke up shortly after.

Two years later I was dating Judith, who had just been chosen Ishpeming Winter Sports Queen in 1952. Of course I attended her crowning ceremony, which was held during a ski tournament at Suicide Hill on—you guessed it—a very cold and blustery day. But she looked down at me from the stand she occupied with her court and sent a smile right past all that frozen purple into the only part of my face that doesn't change color in cold temperatures: my brown eyes.

I knew right then that that was true love, but I didn't take any more chances during our courtship, taking her to inside functions during winter months—at least until after she had said: "I do." I'm still pretty much a warm-weather spectator whenever possible. But if you should see me at a cold-weather event I just couldn't avoid, don't tell me I look cold, because I won't be able to say anything to you by way of response except: "Angh gertz wwig cooln..."

# A Perfect Moment Remembered

∽

I had one of them again last Saturday afternoon. It came upon me suddenly, at least the awareness of it did, and once recognized stayed with me just long enough for me to put a label on it: a perfect moment! I've had a number of them in the sixty-four years I've been rattling around on this planet, but I couldn't tell you anything about the previous ones because it is in the nature of perfect moments that they be recognized, savored, and then filed away into one's subconscious—well-being boosters, if you will, which keep us "up" without our knowing it even after we've forgotten their details.

Before the forgetting process begins with this last perfect moment, I'd like to share it with you. The building blocks for it were being gathered for quite a while so that they could come together at three-thirty last Saturday afternoon. A few weeks ago, while I was ambling about our property looking for signs of deer so that I'd be able to provide an optimistic report to some hunters who use our guest house as their headquarters, I found both the signs and an almost perfectly formed spruce tree that I had somehow overlooked in earlier Christmas tree searches.

This past Saturday, when our luncheon conversation turned to Christmas trees for the first time this season, I remembered that tree, and by three-fifteen I stood in front of it corroborating my initial judgment as to color and shape and then cutting it down with a small pruning saw.

About eight inches of snow had fallen the night before, but the clouds that had brought it had dissipated, to be replaced by a sky that poets sometimes like to call cerulean. The beauty of the day hadn't registered with me yet because I was preoccupied, outgoing, with concerns about whether I'd find that tree again and if, indeed, it would past muster. And the prospect of pulling it about a quarter of a mile through deep snow also had me thinking prosaically instead of poetically.

But, the cut having been made and the tree looking even closer to perfect lying there framed against the snow, I started the return trip, and a pleasant flow of thoughts began as I anticipated the silent applause that Judith would send me from her side of the kitchen window when I stood the tree up outside it later for her imprimatur.

Halfway home I stopped for about the fourth time to take a breather. The early-winter sun was quite low in the sky by this time, and my body cast an elongated shadow somewhat behind me as I faced our house on the hill south of me, still an eighth of a mile away. It occurred to me, looking at that shadow, that it was probably about the same shape as one I would have made more than three decades earlier when I had traversed almost the same path as I pulled the first Christmas tree for our house on the hill toward its rendezvous with the chief tree inspector in our family.

Shadows are really kind, if you think about it: they never reveal wrinkles, gray hair, or any of the other signs of advancing age. I think it was that shadow which triggered the perfect moment, that and my German shepherd dog, Jake, who, in his youthful exuberance, ran circles around me and the tree, nipping playfully at both in hope of getting response from at least one. He had been under house arrest during the deer hunting season because both his size and color made him vulnerable to the errant rifles of hunters returning empty-handed from hunting fields at dusk, so this was a special moment for him, too.

On his sixth circuit I dove for him, and we rolled around together in the snow for a while. I don't know what he shed in the process, but I got rid of fifty years in less than a minute, and I was twelve again, the dog's name was Gyp, and it was my mother who was waiting at home to inspect the tree.

Sun, shadow, snow, and symmetry of tree and of time produced that particular moment, which I hated to have end. But I brushed off my clothing and gathered up those fifty years lying scattered about the snow and arranged them into a configuration that others would recognize. Then I pulled that perfect tree once more toward its and my destination.

# The Evolution of the Kiss

∾

"Styles change." That two-word explanation is trucked out by members of the younger generation to account for any kind of social behavior these days that we on the downhill side of life can't get used to as we observe it—mostly from the sidelines. It was laid on me recently by a youthful relative when I commented upon an on-screen kiss that we both observed as we watched a movie together on TV.

I sensed that those two words represented reflex action on his part and that, deep down, he thought it was ever the same with kissing. So I've decided to make this an informative essay which might shed some light on an activity that is not likely to go away anytime soon and one that most of us have derived pleasure from.

Movies offer a great opportunity to observe kissing, and because I've been watching them in theatres and on my television screen for more than half a century, I think I qualify as an expert on the subject. Back in the days of Greta Garbo and Clark Gable camera angles used by directors for romantic scenes were such that one never really got to see the lips of the participants make contact. Cameras instead zeroed in on the look of rapture and anticipation on the faces of the lovers just prior to the kiss.

Eyes were closed as soon as the faces of the two participants were close enough together to permit a successful instrument approach the rest of the way. Head movements were practically non-existent, and the principals discreetly faded from view after only a few seconds. Actors and actresses were able to "fake it" and quite often did, thus the instructional value of this activity to neophyte kissers in the theater, who hoped to get some practice after the movie ended, was minimal.

Eventually movie directors got really daring and introduced head gyrations which suggested that there was some lip mashing going on, though lip close-ups were still a no-no. The camera was held on the principals a bit longer, and before the still-discreet fadeout, they sometimes made a provocative move or two which hinted at things to come.

There were many stages in the evolution of the kiss which I will leave to other scholars to detail. But in the movies hinting has given way to explicitness that provides excellent instruction indeed to young viewers, at least a few of whom don't wait until the end of the movie to practice what they have just learned.

As for me, I observe, and what I've observed primarily is that today's movie kissers open wider than they do when they go to the dentist, and lip nibbling and more aggressive chewing begin immediately. As far as I've been able to determine, the male works on his partner's upper lip, and she, of course, has no choice but to go for his lower. What this might suggest about continued male dominance over the female I don't dare say.

Many of the same movements used by children in attacking ice cream cones are employed by contemporary kissers. The eyes of the participants usually remain open throughout the activity, apparently the better to gauge the impact of a particular move and maybe to permit a quick medical inspection of one's partner's mouth in these perilous times. Almost without exception these on-screen kisses are followed by some pretty steamy stuff, the degree of steaminess dictating whether the movie will get the much coveted "R" rating or not.

I don't know how all this impacts romantic activity in the real world because I haven't had the opportunity for direct observation, but since it has been said so often that life imitates art (or is it the other way around?), I have to assume some carry-over.

But this I do know: if I ever approached Judith with a gleam in my eye and a wide open mouth, she would immediately stuff a piece of toast, a cookie, or a section of fruit into it—most likely the last because she's on a bit of a health kick these days. Whatever romantic notions might have motivated my approach would be put on hold during the process of chewing and swallowing the proffered food, by which time my mind, with its increasingly short attention span, would have turned to something else.

One final observation: any style of kissing in which it is difficult to tell whether the participants are romantically inclined or just plain hungry cannot last, and before long young folks will once again be able to practice the art of osculation by letting the thumb and forefinger on one hand function as their partner's lips and get good enough at it to avoid embarrassing themselves when their first opportunity for the real thing presents itself.

# Grow Old Along with Me—
## the Natural Way

ॐ

If I ever harbored any doubts about growing old natu-rally, without attempting to thwart nature where super-ficial appearances are concerned, they were dispelled when, within one twenty-four- hour period, I saw both Helen Gurley Brown and Bob Hope on television.

Helen, self-styled leader of sexually liberated old peo-ple, may or may not have had a facelift or two, but her pale skin was stretched so taut over a fleshless skull that, to me, she looked more like a zombie than a living, breath-ing person. On camera she seemed obsessed with con-vincing viewers that the Biblical three score years and ten that she has already been granted upon this earth repre-sented her adolescence and she was still in the bloom of youth. But all I saw was a blossom gone to seed, and her attempts to hide that with hair style, clothing, and makeup only made her look more ridiculous.

Bob, who probably can't even remember when he was seventy, showed up with hair, now grown quite sparse, dyed a color it probably never was naturally—one that ill suited the old face below it. Remembering a recent infomercial in which somebody (with a straight face, believe it or not) spent half an hour trying to sell bald people on the idea of painting their bare pates to match whatever hair they had left, I didn't know whether to laugh or be depressed by the apparent dread of growing old that motivated Hope, Brown, and whoever fell for that paint job.

It is ironic that at a time when most folks can just about count on spending more than a quarter of their years in a stage that was once referred to, with more than a little respect, as "old age," so much time, energy, and money are being spent to deny its existence.

Most of us get through life by dividing it into stages, and we refer to the end of each stage as "the light at the end of the tunnel." For the high school kid it's graduation and getting on with adult things. For parents it's getting those kids grown up and on their own. For workers who've been at it for three decades or so it's their day of retirement.

But then that light goes out and we're put on frantic hold that we're expected to be able to sustain until the day we die. Dr. Ruth tells us that we're supposed to be just as eager for sex at age eighty as we were at twenty, and all those octogenarians for whom that is not the case feel vaguely guilty when, once in bed, all they want to do is go to sleep.

Other experts adjure us to keep on learning new things and offer us all kinds of courses toward that end at local universities. And there's always a Jack LaLanne or his female counterpart with yet another videotape featuring old muscles kept young by a daily regimen of grunting and sweating in front of the tube, followed by a swig of some kind of diet drink "to replace vital fluids" and a teaspoonful or two of minced broccoli, tofu, and low-fat yogurt.

Television programs, newspapers, and the *Reader's Digest* regale us with stories about 100-year-old grandmothers who have climbed the Matterhorn and equally super-annuated folks who have just walked across a stage with their great-grandchildren to accept their high school diplomas.

Worst of all, patent medicine salesmen, now shouting out at us from a TV screen instead of from the back of a wagon, promise us eternal youth if we just buy a bottle of their combination of vitamins, watercress, and rhinoceros horn—just three tablets a day after meals. And plastic surgeons wait in the wings with their tummy tucks, lipo-suction, and other procedures, which they aver will bring back our youth, but of course never do.

I am not opposed to old people's being active and trying to remain in the mainstream of life as long as possible. But they should settle for a spot in that stream where the current is slower. Why can't we be willing to say to those who have been lucky enough to get to age 70 that it's okay to get off the speedboats of life and try for as many years of "old age" as Fate will grant them on rafts that go with the flow.

I think it's time for society to re-introduce some dignity to that last stage of life. Oliver Wendell Holmes said in one of his poems: "If I should live to be the last leaf upon the tree in the spring, let them smile as I do now at the old forsaken bough where I cling." Remember he said "smile," not "snicker". Keep that in mind when this writer boards that raft a few years down the road.

# Don't Bring on the New—I Liked the Old

∾

I had a brief affair a couple of years ago. It began as I walked down the dry-cereal aisle of a local supermarket and saw what was soon to be the object of my affections close to the end of that aisle—clad, if my memory serves me correctly, in autumn gold with white trim. It wasn't love at first sight, but there was an immediate attraction on my part, enhanced when a name, five syllables of beauty and simplicity, impacted my emotions so powerfully that before long we were heading home together.

For a year after that fateful first meeting, we encountered each other regularly, always in the dry-cereal aisle of that supermarket. And all those encounters ended in our going home together. I am convinced that our affair would still be going strong, but one day that object of my affection was not in the accustomed place waiting for the touch of my hand and all that usually followed it.

I can't count how many times I walked in vain down that aisle in the months that followed, looking for that autumn gold and white trim. I did see at least half a dozen one-night stands out of my past, but no "Common Sense Oat Bran," four words that even today fill me with almost unbearable longing.

Okay, so I cheated a little with this slightly salacious introduction, but how many of you would still be reading this essay if you discovered in its first sentence that it was going to be about packaged dry cereal? Anyway, now that you've read this far, why not stay with me, because I DO have a point or two to make.

I have long said that we have too many consumer product choices these days. Nowhere is that made more obvious than on those ever-lengthening dry-cereal shelves in supermarkets. Can anybody out there say with a straight face that our lives have been improved by the availability of more than half a dozen of those cereals with some variation of the words "chocolate" or "cocoa" in their names? Or "honey" or "brown sugar" or "fruit"?....the list goes on. How many different shapes does it make sense for these cereals to come in—how many squares, circles, nuggets, puffs, flakes, etc. will satisfy us and make us think we're in dry cereal heaven?

Well, for me we passed that number years ago. I go through a sort of mini-hell every time I run the gauntlet of those long supermarket cereal lines in search of the four that I grew up with: Kellogg's Corn Flakes, Wheaties, Kix, and Rice Krispies. Fortunately they have not been crowded off the shelves by all those sugary, false-fruity, unrelentingly crisp interlopers, which are packaged—and named—so alluringly that from time to time even a veteran cereal slurper like me, who ought to know better, reaches for one.

That's where the one-night stands come in. You see, I'm in the habit of having a bowl of cereal with my late-evening news—who says life can't be exciting for the Social Security set!—and almost every new one I bring home I find so unpalatable that I can't finish even one bowl of it. I wind up giving it to my dog Jake, muttering apologies under my breath to him as I do so. The rest of the package is consumed by our younger son, Dan. Neither Jake nor Dan has ever met a morsel of food he didn't like, which makes me feel a little better about my cereal-purchasing disasters.

Then one day I discovered Common Sense Oat Bran. I think I have at least a little common sense, and I had been reading a lot about the ability of oat bran to reduce cholesterol. So I gave it a try and found that it combined all the qualities I liked in such a cereal. For a time I WAS in cereal eater's heaven, and going down the cereal aisle in the supermarket stopped being a traumatic experience for me.

It became one again when I could not find it one day and learned from a store employee that it was no longer available. I shouldn't have been surprised. Over the years I have developed quite a list of food items which I liked enough to keep going back for until they were yanked from the shelves forever.

The pattern is always the same: a product disappears and I, unwilling to acknowledge that it's no longer being made, keep looking for it. And whenever we travel, I stop at any unfamiliar supermarket chain along the road to check for it, I was successful with one such search last March, when Judith and I took a brief trip to Panama City, Florida. While she did the serious shopping for groceries (we stayed in a condo there for a week), I drifted over to the dry cereal aisle and—you've probably guessed it—located four packages of my precious Common Sense Oat Bran.

Looking back on that Florida trip, I can honestly say that that discovery was its highlight. A hurricane had pretty well annihilated the beaches in front of our condo a few months before our visit; and it rained for all but one of the days we were there. But I had been reunited with my lost love, if only long enough to consume those four packages, which were probably the last ones on earth!

I would not have had to go through this trauma of permanent separation from something I had grown to like if cereal producers hadn't dangled it in front of me in the first place. I think I could have gone through life quite happily with the seven or eight available back in the late forties. More is not necessarily better. As we double our choices, we halve our pleasure—and quadruple our sense of frustration. Besides, I can't handle many more of these affairs, even if they are of the stomach and not the heart. I'm into permanent relationships these days. At my age "permanent" is not that long!

(Note: I sent a copy of this essay to the W. K. Kellogg Corporation, and a representative from that firm telephoned me to let me know that Common Sense Oat Bran is still available by direct order from the company. So, happily, my "affair" has resumed.)

# Childhood Wages Remembered

∾

After the last leaf fell from the trees in his yard this past fall, an elderly friend of mine who doesn't do leaf raking any more sought out the services of a couple of pre-teen boys to do the job for him. They were more than willing but announced up front that, working together, they expected to receive ten dollars an hour for their services.

Said friend told me he was so shocked by what he construed as their brashness that he sent them on their way and decided to wait for a high wind from the right direction to take care of most of the leaves. He had been prepared to pay them what he considered a fair wage, but he didn't want those young whippersnappers telling him what that was. Then the two of us reminisced about the way it had been when we were kids. He is about fifteen years my senior, but we both had gone through our childhood before WWII, when relationships between children and adults were indeed different from what they are today.

My first legitimate pay for services rendered was a

handful of very sticky candy. Mr. Kehoe, the "big room" teacher in our two-room school, was a great scavenger, who during the summer months would purchase at a huge discount--or perhaps receive free of charge—the candy at the bottom of boxes in Mikuliches' General Store which had become too sticky to sell to the general public.

This he employed to pay us kids for filling his woodbox, raking his yard, or running errands for him. When we had completed an assigned task, we'd knock on his door and wait in respectful silence and anticipation for him to appear with one of those candy boxes, reach into it to grab a mass of the sticky stuff, its size proportionate, in his opinion—which we never questioned—to the job done, and deposit it in our grimy, outstretched hands. We then ran off to consume it at our leisure.

When we became just a bit older he started to pay us in coin, but again our hands were outstretched to receive it, and we never dared to look down to see how much he had paid us until we were out of his sight. Until I took a steady job working in my uncle's sawmill at the age of sixteen, the only time I knew in advance what my rate of pay was to be for any work done for hire was when I peeled railroad ties on a landing in front of our yard or when I picked potatoes for a few pennies a bushel.

We were expected to give the farmer our bushel count at the end of each day, which most accepted as accurate. But the payer was still in control of the situation. I remember one saying to one of my fellow pickers: "You talk lie, me no believe," in the broken English we were not unaccustomed to hearing in our ethnic community, after which he reduced the total by x number of bushels, and that was the end of that transaction. Knowing that particular picker, he probably did "talk lie."

When, as a teenager, I began to hire out as a laborer on threshing crews around Traunik, I could count on earning "folding money," which was placed in those same hands that had earlier accepted sticky candy and small coins. Again, there were no wage negotiations in advance. I knew that when the grain was threshed, a process that on some farms took a couple of days, I could expect fair payment for my work. Fairness was defined slightly differently from farm to farm, but that made payday all the more exciting. There may have been an hourly formula that the farmers employed, but I had no idea what it was.

Mostly, I was just pleased to be working for money once in a while because when I wasn't, I'd be ungainfully employed at home. Besides, I was so filled with self-importance as a threshing crew member that wages didn't seem very significant to me. After all, I was being asked to do manly things like drive the trucks out into the fields to pick up the grain (mostly oats in our area), put a moistened bandanna over my mouth as I spread the straw being blown into the barn, or feed the sheaves of grain onto a conveyor belt, grain side first, which then pulled them into the threshing mechanism. This last job puffed me up the most because I had heard stories, mostly apocryphal, about careless workers falling onto that belt and being chewed up in the machinery, so I felt that during those moments I was truly living life "on the edge."

I don't think I was exploited by any of the people who hired me in my youth and, looking back, I'm grateful that with all the other troubles that attend growing up I didn't have to concern myself with how much money I could earn. There is more than enough time for that in the adult lives of most of us.

As for my elderly friend, I hope he won't have to rely on the wind this time but that a couple of young boys—or girls (leaf raking doesn't require bulging biceps)—will take on the task without asking in advance: "What's in it for me." He told me that he'll give a generous tip to any such

kids who show up and that he won't mind it at all if they do a few belly flops into the leaf piles while they work. From where I sit that seems like a pretty good deal.

# Being Frank Is Not Always Easy

∞

While I was still teaching English, I read about an experiment in which identical student essays were corrected by a group of composition teachers (who didn't know the writers)—identical, that is, except for the fictitious names written at the tops of those essays.

Interesting result: whenever those names were "Lisa," "Janet," "Tom," or "Mark," those essays were generally judged to be better than they were when "Bertha," "Gertrude," "Horace," or "Ralph," (examples mine) were the identifying names. So maybe Shakespeare was wrong after all: a rose by any other name does not necessarily smell as sweet—or at least it's not perceived to.

I got to thinking about that experiment again the other day when I realized that Dave Barry and Mike Royko, to name just a couple of columnists, are published in hundreds of newspapers nationwide while I continue to appear in only two.

About a month ago the publisher of a daily newspaper

in Mattoon, Illinois, got my hopes up by asking my permission (and getting it, of course) to reprint two of my essays that had apparently struck his fancy.

For a couple of weeks thereafter I went about thinking: "Look out, Barry and Royko, here comes Bartol!" Alas, there were no follow-up requests from him or any other publisher, and in trying to figure out why, I finally decided that "Frank" just doesn't have the selling power of "Dave" or "Mike."

You have to bear in mind that writers are generally so enamored of their own words that comparisons based on style and content are inevitably "no contest" in favor of the writer doing the comparing—forget what the rest of the world seems to be saying. So blaming failure on one's name seems logical in that context.

Anyway, I see myself as being too close to the end of my writing career to bother changing my name to "Michael David Bartol." I'll just plug along as good old Frank and take what comes. There are signs on the horizon (which I'll mention below) that my first name may yet become popular—at which point, if I'm still writing, I'll have to come up with some other excuse for not making it big.

My conversations with other folks, all of whom have a name, suggest that people are generally less than totally happy with the ones their parents pick out for them—even Lisa, Janet, Tom, and Mark, who get those good grades on their essays! I don't really dislike mine, but I wish I would have encountered more than just one or two Frank's among the 3,000 students I worked with in thirty years of teaching so I could know how this generation of them is turning out.

It doesn't seem to be much of a young people's name. Those who have it are often known to their peers by a nickname. Mine was "Boy"—I hope because "Boy Bartol" had a nice alliterative ring to it and not because there was a perceived need to verify one particular aspect of my physical being.

I looked into the phone book just now and saw enough "Frank's" to establish that most of us fess up to that first name when we grow up. And there have been some pretty important folks with mine, as well as some with a variant that I'm inclined to claim.

Dedicated political liberal that I am, I'd like to think that FDR's buddies sometimes called him "Frank." And, just maybe, Francis Scott Key was called "Frank" by his friends around the poker table. As for that famous architect, I wish he hadn't insisted upon slipping "Lloyd" between his first and last name. That habit indicated a lack of faith that gets passed on to the rest of us.

My first name hasn't gotten much help from American idiom so far. Every Tom, Dick, and Harry knows that a good Joe can get a Dear John letter and that he'll have to borrow from Peter to pay Paul and work as a Jack of all trades to get his life back to where he's feeling Jim dandy. Where is "Frank" in all this? The comic strips give us "Frank and Ernest," but have you seen the way those two characters are drawn—and portrayed?

There is one medium, though, that is gradually helping to change the image of the name my mom and dad gave me: television. I cannot watch TV for more than an hour without encountering a "Frank" either in the commercials or the programs themselves. Writers are hooked on it for some reason that I can't fathom, and it's getting as common in the make-believe world as it is rare in the real one.

Perhaps those writers know something we don't: that the quintessential name for males of our species deserves to be "Frank," and that eventually it will be the touchstone name for success at just about everything. I hope that happens soon because Mike and Dave are getting farther ahead of me all the time, and, frankly, I'm getting a little despondent about that.

# White Metal Puts Me in a Black Mood

∾

I'm trying to decide whether the words, "heavy metal" or "white metal" have the greater capacity to put me in an ugly mood. Both accomplish that feat quite well, I must say, but I think right now I'm leaning toward the latter, because heavy metal intrudes upon my life only long enough for me to get to the radio to change stations before I have to listen to more than ten notes of that awful music.

But white metal can't be gotten rid of that easily. I am listing a bit to starboard as I write this because one of the casters on my desk chair gave out---for the third time! I'm no longer surprised when this happens, because I learned after the collapse of the first one that white metal is the basic material used in every replacement caster that fits this particular chair.

But I do feel deceived nonetheless, because this caster and most other things made out of white metal (which, by the way, isn't white at all but a light gray) are covered with a finish that makes them appear as if they are constructed of cast iron, stainless steel, aluminum, or brass. The reputation these metals have for strength is naturally transferred to that gray stuff hidden underneath, which I have to assume is the intent of the manufacturers.

I've had enough experiences to validate my conclusions about white metal, another of which I'll share with you here: Several years ago I decided to attach a yard light to the peak of our house so that folks who ventured this far into the boondocks at night could tell whether the tail of the German shepherd dog who guards our property was wagging or not.

Everything went well until I screwed in the swivel unit that holds the bulb. Not wanting to haul the ladder out to tighten it again at some later date, I gave it an extra half turn—and felt that sickening give which told me that I shouldn't have. I stood on that ladder, broken piece in hand, filling the country air with expletives which were separated from each other by the dreaded term "white metal."

What saddens me a little here is the realization that readers under thirty (I hope I have a few of those) won't react to this jeremiad at all, because they have grown up knowing that what you see is not necessarily what you get when you buy something that is advertised as being made of metal.

Making things look like something they ain't is pretty much the name of the game in manufacturing these days. That's why a rabbit that was hippity hopping across U.S. 41 a while back did several hundred dollars damage to the grille of my car when he made contact with it at the top of one of those hops. Underneath a thin layer of chrome on that grille was plastic, white metal's "right hand man" in the business of manufacturing deception.

Older guys, who served their repair and handyman apprenticeship in the 50's or before, can identify with all this, I'm quite sure. Back then we had to contend only with real metal, and we could tighten down bolts and screws until they just wouldn't move any more. Disasters like the one I had with my yard light just couldn't happen.

Maybe Henry Sipila, legendary blacksmith of my area before my time, could have sheared a bolt with the strength of an arm accustomed to wielding a huge hammer to beat hot steel into submission. But we mere mortals tackled all our jobs of attaching part A to part B secure in the knowledge that we'd run out of strength before the metal we were working with did.

I liked that feeling. It's one I get today only when I "monkey around" with our old Ford tractor, which my dad bought back in 1945, and with the implements that came with it. To loosen bolts on that equipment I sometimes have to put a pipe extension on my wrench, and I often employ the same technique in tightening them again. And I never shear them off!

I don't expect manufacturers to change their ways as a result of anything I say here, but I wish I could get them to put a warning label—warning labels are very fashionable these days—on all bolts, screws, and other things made of white metal. Recommended wording: "White metal employed here. Tighten at your own risk." That might help guys like me just a little.

# I'll Take Arvo over Sam Any Time

∽

Acouple of miles west of downtown Marquette one of the behemoths of modern merchandising, Wal-Mart, is about to open its doors to central Upper Peninsula shoppers. Twenty-five miles to the southeast, one of the last holdouts of another era of marketing, the Unity Co-op of Eben Junction, is about to give up the ghost.

A lot of hoopla will attend the first event, with hundreds of people lining up on grand opening day to grab one of those items which such enterprises usually offer "far below cost" on such occasions to lure folks in, where, if all goes according to plan, those folks will buy other items at inflated prices to make up for those "specials."

And local entrepreneurs will continue to state publicly that they welcome yet another example of our grand free enterprise system to the area even as they privately wring their hands at the looming spectre of more monuments to it in the form of abandoned malls and store buildings, some of which will undoubtedly turn out to be their own.

Not too many people will pay attention to the demise of the Unity Co-op. It has been hanging on bravely in the face of competition from other Wal-Mart-type businesses for the past two decades, one of the last of its kind here in this area—or anywhere else in the U.S. for that matter.

Its management adhered to a merchandising principle which worked very well for a long time: service to the customers paid for through modest mark-ups on all the products that passed through its doors.

Some merchants abused that old system, of course, charging whatever the traffic would bear. But, for the most part, there was an honest simplicity to that way of doing business which is considerably harder to find under those 200,000-square-foot roofs which have become the hallmark of the modern way.

I was never a storekeeper myself, but I rubbed elbows with many of them over the years. My growing-up experience was mostly with Mikuliches' Store in Traunik, where just about everything we needed was for sale but nothing was ever "on sale."

We liked it that way, and because we knew we'd find the same situation at any of the ten or so other general stores within a dozen miles of Traunik, we never had to trouble ourselves with the kind of bargain shopping that makes "going to the store" such a frenzied and frustrating activity today.

What those old stores gave us was the human contact which is so conspicuously absent from most big stores now, no matter how many folks are hired to stand at their entrances with smiles pasted on their faces as they welcome us in and thank us for shopping there as we leave.

Some have even given up on going through the motions, succumbing totally to scanners, computers, and other substitutes for real live employees. Last week, at a gas station in a Chicago suburb, I bought gasoline for my car without ever seeing another human being on the service side.

I shoved my credit card into a slot and then almost immediately saw a message on the screen which most politely referred to me by name and "personally" asked me to wait a moment before giving me instructions as to how to proceed from there. When I hung up the hose later, the pump disgorged my receipt, and I left that station with a full tank but empty spirits.

Whenever I went to the Unity Co-op, however, I was greeted first by Betty Salo, who divided her time between working the check-out counter and stocking shelves, after which I walked back to the heart of the store, where, if I was lucky—which was most of the time—I'd find my old school mate, Arvo Hakkola, the store manager, who took his turn at just about every other job there, too.

The biggest loss when the Unity Co-op closes won't be convenient access to merchandise down the road, because at least for the time being the Chatham Co-op is there to provide that, but convenient access to Arvo and the homespun philosophy and wisdom he dispensed with every nut, bolt, stove pipe, etc. that he sold. I always felt better leaving than coming, even when Arvo and I had just agreed that the outside world was indeed going to Hell in a handbasket.

Arvo told me that he expects to be kept busy running a portable sawmill when he closes the store, but I don't need to have logs sawed nearly as often as I need to pick up a bag of cement or two, which he keeps in stock just because he knows his customers need the product from time to time. I suspect that he throws away several sacks every year after the cement in them has hardened to the point where it can't be used any more and in so doing throws away any hope for profit on that particular product.

So on Saturday I stocked up on as much of Arvo's com-

mentary as he had time to give me to tide me over until we meet again. The cement I passed on because I knew it would harden up in the sack in my garage. But not Arvo's good humor and gentle disposition. I expect that to remain fresh in my mind for some time to come—and I don't look to find a reasonable substitute for it at most of the other places I shop in these days.

# We Need Old Things and New Attitudes

ᖗ

"Baraka" is an Arabic word which refers to the value that adheres to an item because of its long use by an individual or a family. That term never got into the English language even way back when just about everybody could point to at least half a dozen things at home which contained that quality, so it is unlikely to find its way into the dictionary now that we are firmly mired in a throwaway culture which prizes few things that are more than a year or so old.

I find it sad to realize that there aren't very many family heirlooms any more, or even keepsakes, as items of lesser value were sometimes called. People are fighting over a lot of things these days but not very much about who gets what when the old folks die and the family home has to be broken up. The only fighting that ensues after that sad event is about how the proceeds from the inevitable garage sale that follows hard upon the funeral are to be divvied up.

This absence of baraka is at least partly due to technology. "State of the art" has become the criterial term in defining the value of anything today. The mechanical and electronic appliances which dominate the furnishings of most households are on the way to obsolescence almost as soon as they leave the store and thus are not likely to acquire baraka, and the rest of the household furnishings are built to fall apart faster than the folks who use it.

It was not always that way, even in my lifetime. My parents bought a Pullman sofa (I don't think that brand name even exists today) shortly after WWII, the frame of which was so solidly put together that the upholsterer who refurbished it about twenty years ago practically caressed it as he worked, lamenting at the same time that "they just don't make them like that any more." That sofa is still in use at the home place, and because we've pretty much agreed that it will continue to be the "home place" far into the future, no decisions regarding it will have to be made for a long time. But if plans change, I hope a few of my descendants will fight over it—just a little.

I'm into baraka myself, and there are quite a few things in our house that are valuable to me simply because I've been using them for a long time, most of them inconsequential items that wouldn't command much money at a garage sale, if indeed they would sell at all.

The first that comes to mind is an old wooden spoon that we have had in our kitchen ever since we were married forty-one years ago. Noting its decrepit appearance and suspecting that it has increased its capacity to harbor bad bugs and chemicals over the years in spite of her efforts to keep it clean, Judith has bought me replacements for it from time to time. But they just sit in the receptacle we have for such items next to our sink, looking prim, proper, and shiny new, while I push them aside to reach for old faithful. I like the feel of every part of that old spoon, from its handle to what goes into my mouth as I test the soup or stew I've been stirring with it. I hope that when I die some family member will remember my affection for that battered wooden utensil and transfer it with tender loving care to his kitchen. I think it's good for at least twenty more years, but I'm not so sure I am.

Baraka has not been easy to attain with any item in our house because Judith is just not into keeping old things around too long (she has been giving me some strange looks lately), but I see signs that that may be changing. Two years ago she bought a bowl at a pottery shop in Ishpeming, which she has been using daily ever since to eat her breakfast bowl of Wheaties from. It reposes in a special place of honor when not in use, on our dining room table (which is also our kitchen table), next to the centerpiece there. She washes, rinses, and dries it separately immediately after breakfast. That is a solemn ritual, and I try not to engage in idle chatter while it's going on.

One day when she was distracted for a moment, I put that bowl into the sink with the rest of the dirty dishes and found out from her reaction to my doing so how special it is to her. That pleases me. Maybe someday a pottery bowl and an old wooden spoon can together trigger memories of two people who used them long enough to give them that special value called baraka.

By my definition, baraka is most valid when attached to an object of insignificant monetary value which someone wants to keep just to remain connected with his own or his family's past. We all need a few such things around now that disconnecting seems to be so much the order of the day in our society.

# Dogs and Men: Some Parallels?

ɔ

J ust before deer hunting season began last fall a spike-horn buck crossed the road a couple of hundred feet east of our driveway into the path of a vehicle, thereby denying the hunters that were to come to our place later the opportunity to do him in. At least I assume that's what happened. I discovered the deer's carcass at least a week after his demise when I noticed that our German shepherd, Jake, made a beeline for a spot in the woods about fifty feet from the road whenever he had a chance to and returned about an hour later looking totally satiated and contented.

I had no problem with his filling his stomach without emptying our dog food bin, but when he decided to make his cache a way station for exploration farther from home, I hooked the carcass to my pickup and dragged it to a field behind our house, where Jake could gnaw away on what remained of it after the ravens discovered it and still be in sight of our place.

Four months later he continues working on it, but when

it was small enough for him to manage an improvement upon our earlier move, he dragged it up to his favorite tree right outside our kitchen window. I left him there just a few minutes ago sulking because I wouldn't grab the other end of a hunk of deer hide to play tug of war with him. But like his master, he has a very forgiving disposition, and I'm quite sure he's out there right now engaged in the primordial pleasure of demolishing one of the last bones of that spikehorn buck.

When we bought Jake, we were given a sheet of paper outlining his pedigree. Apparently breeders over the generations had been working hard to produce an animal with the "proper" temperament, size, color, and bone structure. Looking at Jake as one of the outcomes of their work, they would be quite satisfied, because he is a handsome animal and very gentle.

But it is when I see him by that tree, completely oblivious to temperatures as low as twenty below as he chews on those deer bones or curled up in a ball asleep as snow almost completely covers him, that he gives me the greatest pleasure, because in doing those things he is telling me that no matter what man has tried to do to him, nurturally and genetically, he has not been able to eradicate his essential dogness. I like that because I see a parallel here between dog and man that makes me more hopeful about the future of the latter.

Jake is not impervious to the lure of creature comforts when they are offered him. The same dog who can be so disdainful of cold can also scratch on our backdoor imploring to be let into the house to lie on his blanket in our entryway. And he is content, much of the time, with multicolored dry dogfood called Kibbles 'n Bits and half a chocolate chip cookie for dessert (Yes, I know that chocolate is bad for him!).

But from time to time Canis familiaris becomes once

again his cousin Canis lupus, and I am reminded that perhaps there is also an essential man-ness to which we at least have the potential to return. Today, spoiled by air conditioners, central heating systems, and insulated clothing that keeps us warm from head to toe, we can survive only within very narrow ranges of temperature.

But at the first annual Outhouse Races in Trenary last year, when the temperature hovered just barely above zero, I watched a couple of guys walk around with heads uncapped and hands unmittened, a beer in one hand and a bratwurst-filled bun in the other, as oblivious to the cold as Jake is when he's working on his deer bones outside our window, and that told me there is hope for us, even though I watched most of those races through the windshield of my pickup—with the motor running and the heater going full blast!

Buying into the notion that much of what I see about me today is nothing more than a palimpsest which, scraped away, will return us to the beginning, as it were, makes today easier to take. I have long ago concluded that society as we now know it is moving inexorably toward its eventual destruction. Technology is doing more to us than for us, and our behavioral response to it is turning us into something that many of us don't want to be.

But Jake gives me hope that when it all comes crashing down around us, we'll shake ourselves off, take a backward look at where we have ended up, and then start all over again, making sure we stop somewhere short of that point next time around.

# Old Words, New Meanings
# Make Me Unhappy

ॐ

"Cat ingredients found along Iron County roads." When I read that headline in Saturday's newspaper, my mind immediately conjured up the image of various parts of a cat's anatomy scattered along those roads: a paw here, some whiskers there, a few feet of entrails somewhere else. That image lasted long enough for me to start the day off with a laugh—which I have read countless times is good for my general health. But when it disappeared I was left with a frown on my face— which I have read an equal number of times is bad for my general health—as I realized that only a guy with more than a few miles on his brogans could see the humor (admittedly gruesome) in that headline.

Young newspaper readers thought immediately about the drug presently being produced in the U.P. which "cat" is a shortened name for. After all, more's the pity, their entire lives have been spent in a world in which illicit drugs of various kinds have become almost as American as apple pie.

All this got me thinking about how many perfectly good words, as well as the images those words generate, have been forever changed by this practice of attaching new, usually unfavorable, meanings to them. True, semantic changes have been occurring as long as man has been using language. I would not, today, like to be called "silly," but one of my ancestors, several hundred years ago, would have been pleased, because that word is derived from the Germanic one, "selig," which means "holy." But I WOULD like to be called "nice," as hackneyed as that adjective is, even though that same ancestor would be offended by a word derived from one which meant "not knowing," or, if you will, "ignorant," which survives in the not-so-common present-day English word "nescient."

These last changes occurred over centuries and thus caused no problems for users of English. But the use of a comfortable old word like "cat" to represent something uncomfortable and new doesn't sit very well with me. I wish the coiners responsible for this would have chosen to name the drug "theno," employing contiguous letters just down the line from "cat" in "metcathenone," introducing thereby a completely new word— an appropriately unpleasant-sounding one—instead of corrupting one that heretofore generated warm feelings in feline fanciers everywhere, and in the general population for that matter.

When I was a kid I'd often go down to Mikuliches' General Store in Traunik for a nickel bag of candy, and sometimes I'd sit outside that store and eat it, perhaps washing it down with Coke. I resent whoever it was who did violence to my memories of those halcyon days by using the term "nickel bag" to refer to five dollars' worth of marijuana (or $500, I'm not sure). And the double entendre in the spoken version of the slogan, "Things go better with Coke," which generates knowing snickers from today's sophisticates, increases the level of that resentment

175

a notch or two.

I'd be a lot happier if we'd all try harder to call new things by new names. With old words dying all the time (it's been a very long time since I've used—or seen—the word "whiffletree"), we shouldn't be so reluctant to come up with replacements or so eager to hang yet another meaning on already-overburdened words.

Without being judgmental about homosexuality, I must say we were cheated out of a perfectly good word when "gay" was called into service to stand for a male homosexual. Just think of all the phrases—"the gay nineties," "in gay Paris," "a gay old time"—that we can no longer use with ease.

And why couldn't we have limited the term "seniors" to high school students who, after twelve years in our educational system, have finally achieved that rank, or to those in their last year of college. It annoys me to see a headline reading: "Seniors head for Florida" and learn that the term is referring to a group of old people. I was a senior twice in my life, and I don't ever want to be one again.

I can't imagine Robert Browning writing: "Become a senior citizen along with me, the best is yet to be..." But his invitation to me to "grow old along with me..." is appealing, and I hope I get there before somebody comes up with still another word for the stage of life which I'm now approaching.

# Men, Too, Are Fashion's Slaves

❦

W hen I reached adulthood back in the late 40's, men could ridicule women for the slavish way they jumped through the hoops held up for them by so-called fashion experts without running the risk of having some of their own hoop-jumping activities thrown in their faces. I say that even though, back in 1950, I bought a suit called a one-button roll (or was it "row"?), a neither-fish-nor-fowl mongrel garment that I regretted having purchased almost as soon as I got it home.

After that brief capitulation to men's clothing designers, who were just beginning to test the waters as it were, I and most of my contemporaries went back to more conventional single- and double-breasted suits, and the one-button whatever hung unused at the back of our closets.

While we men sanely selected new clothes only when pants became shiny and jacket elbows wore out, women were replacing their wardrobes every year to try to keep up with designers who moved hemlines up, down, and sideways, added pleats, removed pleats, and shifted waistlines north or south of the equator to produce, among other things, something called the "empire" look, pronounced "om-peer," a word whose sound was decidedly more sexy than the appearance of most of the women who wore clothing featuring it.

But back in the 70's the first sign that the fashion world was going to have its way with us men, too, appeared when lapel, belt, and necktie widths began changing just about every year, and cuffs on trousers disappeared, reappeared, and disappeared again—and some guys, not me, I'm proud to say, started to go for the bait, though I must confess to falling from the ranks of truly independent dressers once in recent years—and I blush even as I write this—when I took my favorite suit coat to a tailor and spent twenty dollars having its lapels narrowed to conform to the fashion of that particular year.

Of late, men's surrender to fashion manipulators has become practically a route, as witness the kinds of trousers (I use the term "trousers" as loosely as many of them fit) some of our younger brethren have been waddling around in. It's not hard for me to imagine that some clothing cabal, meeting in a penthouse somewhere in New York City, decided to find out if we men were really down for the count by commissioning clothing dye manufacturers to come up with a color for those trousers and other clothing so nauseating that men of reason would recoil from it in horror. They figured that if clothing dyed that color would sell, then future manipulation of the male in the clothing market place would be a piece of cake.

It's not any harder for me to imagine further that a dye expert chanced upon some cheese dip that had been at the back of a refrigerator for months past its expiration date and had a flash of inspiration to duplicate the color of the fungus that grew on its surface. There is as yet no name, at least none that I've heard, for that color. It's somewhat like khaki, but to call it that would be an insult to our military. It's not quite yellow, not quite, green, not quite tan, not quite anything. But, whatever it is, it's selling well indeed at the moment, and some of the truly "in" guys here in the U.P., a place that I now realize I had been inaccurately referring to as the last bastion of the truly independent, can now be seen in no other color.

They don't seem to be at all concerned that the only complexion it is in harmony with is that of a guy in the last stages of liver disease or that it could hang on a rack in an army surplus story and make the khaki items next to it look lively, or that it clashes with just about every other color in spite of being so neutral as to make anyone wearing it a non-person. The only time I saw a more blah color was when one of my uncles mixed all the colors in a packet of Easter egg dyes together, reasoning that if they were pretty separately, they ought to be even more so together. They weren't!

I saw a newscast on television the other night in which the co-anchors and all the male reporters were similarly adorned in suits of that non-color, which really depressed me, because it demonstrated that we are now quite obviously putty in the hands of the garment industry, to be molded and shaped by it the way women have been for years. If you wonder where that might take us eventually, go for a walk through the women's section of a department store—if you have the stomach for it. Or better yet, try the men's department in some fashionable place like Saks Fifth Avenue and see what kinds of neckties male shoppers are willing to shell out up to a hundred dollars for!

# Hugging and Patting: Some Observations

∾

A few years ago, I suddenly noticed that an elderly relative of mine used the expression "You know—see" in almost every sentence he uttered. I suppose he had done so for years before it caught my attention, but once it did, I was forever thereafter incapable of ignoring it, and the harder I tried to do so the more it stood out.

In like manner I have watched people hug each other for years, but only recently did I observe that most hugs were accompanied by pats on the back of the one being hugged and quite often on the hugger's back also.

Now, whenever I see two people move toward each other to engage in that ritualistic clinch that we've decided to call a hug—which, by the way, is derived from the Scandinavian word "hugga," meaning "to soothe—I immediately move into position to count the pats. And when I find myself directly involved in hugging, I tend to be preoccupied with what I do with my hands during the event. Naturally, I strive mightily not to pat my partner, but I'm not sure I succeed every time. In any event, the spontaneity of the act and the emotions that should attend it have been getting lost during what I hope is just a phase I'm going through.

I've decided that as long as I can't ignore these pats, I ought to make a scientific study of them. Perhaps any conclusions I might reach will be useful to psychologists, sociologists, and even the legal profession somewhere down the road.

I've already come up with a few hypotheses, whose validity I'll have plenty of opportunities to test because I have a tendency to cling stubbornly to any obsessions that I fasten on to. I kept counting the "you know—see's" of that elderly relative until he died.

Here are some of things I've noticed: there seems to be a connection between the rapidity of the pats during a hug and the affection the two participants have for each other. People who truly like each other pat quite gently, but I once watched two people who I know can hardly stand each other hug, and they patted with such intensity and speed that I at first thought each was trying to dislodge a particle of food from the other's throat.

Of course, one's comfort level with the process of hugging is also a factor in that speed and intensity. I have a relative (my clan is large, so many of my observations are of the "in house" kind) who just doesn't like to hug people, no matter how fond she is of them. When she cannot escape the clutches of a hugger, she, too, pats quite rapidly, but her efforts tend to be irregular and tentative and seem to be signaling that she desperately wants to unclinch.

Stylistic differences in back patting are interesting to note, too. I've seen it done quite gracefully, with the patter strumming his partner's back as if his/her spine represented the strings of a harp. Some patters use wrist action only, their arms and shoulders remaining perfectly still. Others, mostly men, swing from the elbow or even the shoulder.

People usually use the hand they write with when they pat, but I've observed a couple of ambidextrous patters who alternate hands and a few who apply both hands at once—though the latter look so awkward doing it that I can hardly bear to watch.

I trust that no one reading this will be reluctant to do studies of his own in this area. There is plenty of material for everyone. And before you ridicule the whole idea, keep in mind that a professor with the unlikely last name of Birdwhistle catalogued many other gestures that people engage in as they interact. I think it was he who concluded that folks who cross their legs toward each other when seated are making themselves receptive to communication, while those who cross them away from each other are signaling distrust and a lot of other bad things.

Certainly hugging and patting can be more fun to watch than crossed legs. Besides, people are doing a good deal of coming and going these days, so hugging is going on almost everywhere you turn.

If you're too impatient to wait for it to happen in the natural scheme of things, just accept the next invitation to a cocktail party. Most people attending those dismal events hug anything that moves, so you should be kept busy taking notes.

# Full of Baloney and Proud of It

∾

S omebody told me the other day that he thought I was full of baloney and was somewhat surprised when my only response was "thank you." Of course, I knew what he had in mind, but at worst (or should I have said "wurst"?) most people would consider that a friendly insult, and I, who have always enjoyed eating the stuff, didn't feel insulted at all.

The original spelling of the word was "bologna," from the town in Italy where that sausage originated, I presume. But I like the pronunciation spelling of "baloney," and I trust the purists among my readers won't mind my employing it here.

However it is spelled, it is the lunch meat that most of us who carried our lunch to school before WW II would find in our sandwiches, so I suppose nostalgia is at least in part responsible for my affection for baloney—though I know that what fosters nostalgia can also breed contempt and that plenty of my contemporaries have an "I'll never eat baloney again" attitude.

In today's supermarkets there are at least two dozen luncheon meats to choose from, but when as a kid I went down to Mikuliches' General Store and one of the Mikuliches yanked open the heavy oak door of the meat room refrigerator, I peered in to see only three: baloney, salami, and liver sausage. I usually pointed to the baloney, which was then thrown onto a butcher's block, where a chunk approximating the amount requested was cut from it. Slicing of lunch meat was done at home until Mikuliches' went modern and ordered a motor-driven slicer.

The first time I watched that slicer in operation remains clearly etched in my mind though it happened almost half a century ago. Several slices of baloney were peeled off without incident, and I marveled at what a clever little invention that slicer was. But then, as Bob Mikulich pushed the meat against the whirling blade of the machine, his hand slipped, and the blade demonstrated that it didn't care what kind of meat was offered it as it cut a neat path alongside the bone from the tip of one finger to the palm. I remember driving him to a doctor in Gladstone for emergency treatment.

Such an experience could have generated a negative image of baloney for me, but it didn't. When we returned from the doctor's office, I'm fairly sure that Bob or someone else at the store took care of my order of baloney, which I then took home for my mother to work her magic with. Prosaic fare that it was, the magic thus worked was modest, but it was worked often because—and I know this will come as a shock to some people—fried baloney served as the entree for meals at our house as frequently as beef, pork, or chicken.

I don't know what my mother fried it in, perhaps fat rendered from the home-cured bacon we had around most of the time, but if right today a restaurant offered me a choice between filet mignon and a plateful of my mother's fried baloney, I'd choose the latter without hesitation. I can still see those half circles of baloney curling up as they fried and turning a rich brown in those places where the meat made direct contact with the cast iron of the pan.

Placed alongside a bed of rice or mashed potatoes, with maybe creamed carrots and peas for color, leaf lettuce from our garden on the side, and a glass of cold tea to wash it all down, that baloney was meat as good as meat gets for me.

For old time's sake I still occasionally fry up a few slices, but it's not the same. I may be wrong, but I think the baloney of my youth had more meat in it and less cereal. Even if it didn't, I'm afraid that all the warnings about nitrites, salt, fat, etc. in most lunch meats make it hard for me to approach any of them without a sense of guilt for having done so.

All that aside, I believe it was easier for a person to develop a strong liking for something when I was a boy because we weren't overwhelmed by choice the way we are today. That helped make life relatively stress free. Ask today's kids to name a favorite lunch meat and they'll practically have a nervous breakdown deciding, especially now that the already large number available to them is in the process of doubling with the addition of the hyphenated kinds—turkey this and turkey that—which are being introduced to keep that market strong in a health-conscious society.

I refuse to buy turkey-baloney, no matter how much better it is supposed to be for me. To do so would be to sully my memory of the real thing. For your part, the next time something I say annoys you, don't tell me I'm full of baloney. There are several things you might accuse me of being full of that would have the effect you desire. But say "baloney" to me and all you'll get is a smile—as I remember.

# A Private Roadway,
# a Public Remembering

∾

My father could not have known back in 1915 or thereabouts that he and the work crew that he had just been named foreman of were engaged in a construction project that would have a dramatic impact upon the last two years of his life. That project: the building of a railroad spur into the timber-rich area just west of the Soo Line Railroad in what would, a few years later, become the little village of Traunik.

Of course, back then, much of the U.P. was "timber rich," and spurs like the one he was working on were the byways and the main railroad lines the highways on which that timber was hauled to sawmills in places like Gladstone and Escanaba.

None of those spurs had rails on them for very long. When the timber was hauled out so were the tracks, to be laid down again elsewhere. The cut-over land was usually sold to some of the same people who had done the cutting, spur building, and other work associated with the logging industry.

My father bought the forty acre plot of land that "his" spur bisected in 1925 and by the following spring had built a modest home—a shack really—to which he brought his bride, my mother, following a pattern established by most of his lumberjack-turned-landowner contemporaries. By 1929 he had built our permanent family home, in which my mother still lives.

Over the years, that railroad spur was much used to drive our cows to and from a pasture at its terminus, and, growing up, I walked on it often to my favorite fishing spot alongside the remnants of a bridge which took that spur across Dexter Creek. Judith and I built a summer place which has now become our permanent home on a hill overlooking that spot, and I can see it from my office window as I write this.

That railroad grade became the connector between our house and that of my parents a third of a mile away. I drove on it frequently with my Ford tractor, creating with its tires a nice two-rut road that, during the dry season, could be traversed by auto. A decade ago we turned it into an almost-all-season road (we didn't plow it in the winter) by having about a dozen truckloads of gravel spread over it.

Until two years before my father's death at age one hundred, my tractor and my pickup were the vehicles most often driven along our new "highway," my father preferring to use the government-provided road that took him south to the intersection in downtown Traunik and then west to our driveway. But, alert though he was almost up until the moment of his death, he was nevertheless becoming forgetful enough to become a potential menace to others on that public road.

Fortunately, using the only argument I thought would work with him—an economic one—I was able to convince him not to renew his driver's license and to confine his driving from then on to Bartol Highway 101. "After all, dad," I said to him, "you built that road eighty years ago, and you invested some of your money in the graveling project, so it's time you got some benefit from it."

After that I could hear the roar of the motor on his 1984 Buick Skyhawk (he saw no reason to invest in a new muffler for such "off road" use of his car) at least twice a day, as he started it up at home. And, about five minutes later he emerged from the woods just east of our driveway and used up another minute and a half to cover its 300-foot length to the front of our garage.

He always emerged from his car like a man who had just covered a substantial number of miles in it, a bit of self deception which his snail-like pace made easier for him. And very rarely did he acknowledge that he was being restricted to that one-third mile of railroad grade. From time to time he would say to me: "One of these days I want you to take me into Munising so I can renew my driver's license," and I would reply that I was ready to do so at a command from him that both of us knew would never come.

When that brief stretch of railroad spur wasn't quite enough to satisfy his urge to travel by car, he'd turn right off it and onto a field that he and I had cleared together when I was a high school student. That trip would occupy him for a good fifteen minutes because it always included a stop to see how the white spruce trees I had planted more than twenty years ago on a portion of that field were growing.

The arrival of the first snow didn't stop my dad from using his private highway, but he grudgingly put his car away after I had to rescue it once or twice with my tractor. He did so for the last time in November of 1995.

I am certain that that little stretch of railroad-spur-turned-roadway helped motivate him to hang around for his hundredth birthday, and I'm equally certain that every time he rode on it, he remembered one incident or another from its building so long ago. Perhaps, as he did his remembering, he fully expected to see a spur engine with its load coming down the track toward him as he drove. Maybe that's what put him into the ditch the last time I pulled him out.

One thing I'm confident went through his mind often as he reminisced was a sense of pride that way back when he was a stripling of twenty or so, somebody had enough confidence in him to make him foreman on a project that may have seemed modest at the time but produced the most important stretch of road he ever traveled on.

# Remembering My Father A Year Later

❧

Aweek ago Thursday was the first anniversary of my father's death. It was not a day of mournful remembering for me, because my father had lived more than a hundred years, had had a full and rewarding life right up to the end, and had left this world so quietly and peacefully that there was little trauma in his departure that would make me look back upon it with hurt.

But there WAS remembering, enhanced by my going to an upstairs bedroom closet in the home place in search of a box of really old photographs, which I had hoped to browse through by way of honoring him that day. I didn't find that box (the home place has many nooks and crannies into which it may have been placed long ago), but leaning against the wall of the closet was something which said more about my father than any old photos could: a pair of crutches which I had used when recovering from a broken leg at the age of eight.

My father had made those crutches, as he had made, repaired, modified, and built all sorts of things as needed to stretch dollars—and even pennies—during those Great Depression years of my growing up. I remember so clearly his walking in from the garage, where he had spent a couple of hours fashioning them, and handing them to me with a look of pride and satisfaction on his face.

They weren't very fancy, having been shaped with hand tools and smoothed only enough to protect my hands from slivers. But I took them from him eagerly and proceeded to take my first step with their help. The next thing I knew, my father was picking me up off the floor, his look of pride replaced by one of consternation as he realized that the wooden ends of those crutches had immediately slid out from under me on the slippery linoleum-covered floor of our kitchen.

Without a word, he grabbed those crutches and disappeared into the garage once more, where he fashioned rubber ends for them from some inner tube material. They worked well thereafter, and I suspect, without my being aware of it at the time, that experience represented the first installment of a lesson my father reinforced for me throughout his life: never buy what you can make yourself, never throw something away if it's still fixable, and if you get it wrong the first time, go and do it over.

Seeing those crutches again reminded me of so many other examples of my father's resourcefulness. In 1935 he bought a motorized (electrical) reciprocating water pump to replace the hand pump in use at our house until then, and he kept that pump running for more than fifty years, sometimes shaping replacement parts for it from shoe leather and other materials which could always be found hanging from one hook or other in his garage.

Throughout his life he derived his greatest pleasure from resurrecting something that someone else in the family had pronounced ready for the scrap heap. When the muffler on one of his vehicles became noisy, he drove it up on a ramp and got underneath it with sheetmetal, baling wire, and asbestos cement in hand to repair the muffler, often repeating the procedure several times before finally buying its replacement.

One day I threw away a galvanized garbage can that I had been using as an ash can. In spite of the galvanizing, its bottom had pretty much corroded away. A couple of days later, Dad marched triumphantly up our sidewalk carrying that can, for which he had shaped a new bottom out of wood covered by metal so that we could continue using it for ashes.

After his death, I went into his garage several times with the intention of removing from its walls and shelves all those materials he had placed there against the time when he could employ them for yet another repair job. But so far I've always elected to leave them where they are. Wire was his favorite repair material, and there are pieces of various lengths—single strand and woven, copper, steel, and aluminum—hanging there. And pieces of pipe, scraps of sheet metal, nuts, bolts, hinges, brackets—all of them there because, as he would so often say: "You never know when they might come in handy."

I'm well aware that not only my father has passed on but also the era when his kind of seat-of-the-pants, learn-as-you-go techniques for making and repairing things could be employed. He said to me often during the last decade of his life that he just didn't fit in any more.

I think he felt this way at least in part because not much that broke during that last decade was fixable with any of the stuff that he had hanging in his garage. Things had become too electronic, too complex, to be made whole again with a piece of wire, a scrap of sheet metal, and some solder or asbestos cement. And, of course, inevitably, he had lost the ability to make them whole anyway as he approached his hundredth birthday.

That's why I felt only a little sweet-sadness last week as I commemorated the anniversary of his passing by going into his garage for a piece of copper wire, which I then employed to put a splint on a broken snowshoe frame instead of running over to Iversons in Shingleton for a new pair, as it had been my first inclination to do. I think it was a nice tribute to him, and I'm sure it would have pleased him to know that at least a few of the lessons he had taught me survived him.

# Statistics and Pancakes

∾

I often wonder whether I would have been as skeptical about the validity of statistics if it hadn't been for my mother's pancakes and those of my aunt, who lived right next door to us when I was growing up.

Pancakes were on the breakfast menu at our two houses quite often during those Great Depression years, quite possibly because we didn't have to go to the grocery store for the eggs and milk which went into them, and the flour, baking powder, sugar, and salt—which we DID have to go to the store for—didn't dent the food budget very much. Nor did the syrup, which my mother bought in half-gallon cans and which had the flow characteristics of No. 30 motor oil on a sub-zero day and thus was applied sparingly to those pancakes by us in our impatience to start eating them.

Our mothers undoubtedly shared the recipe for pancake batter, so, blindfolded, I could not have told whose I was eating. But they did not go to the same store to buy the griddles on which they were baked, or, if they did, they decided not to be copy-cat purchasers, with the result that the one at our house was circular and about twelve inches in diameter, and the one next door was rectangular and a bit larger.

What could any of that have to do with statistics, you are probably asking at this point. A lot! Our griddle lent itself to the making of one large pancake at a time, the one next door, to four, which were larger than a silver dollar but puny indeed when placed next to the frisbee-sized ones my mother produced.

Of course, they never WERE placed next to each other, and all comparisons were made after breakfast, when they were packed into my stomach and that of my cousin Louie, who was my age and with whom I played—and sometimes fought—almost every day. Louie never tired of telling me that he had consumed X number of pancakes for breakfast, the X standing for a number that to me verged on the astronomical, compared to the five or six of my mother's which I could consume on one of my hungrier days.

These invidious distinctions were being made when we were about eight, an age when technicalities never get in the way of the bottom line as far as bragging rights are concerned. Of course I called his attention to the difference in the size of the pancakes, but he shrugged it off as essentially irrelevant. The truth was that he could eat fifteen pancakes to my five, and that was that. Had the situation been reversed, I would have gloated about my pancake-eating superiority as enthusiastically as he did.

I tried to get my mother to become involved in the matter by making a batch of silver-dollar-sized pancakes just once so that I could zing him with a number that would make his look as insignificant as mine usually did, but she wouldn't go along with it, knowing that our little pancake war would end a lot sooner if she stayed out of it.

197

I THOUGHT YOU'D NEVER ASK!

It did. But the lesson I learned from it never has. I think that, largely because of those pancakes, I grew up being suspicious of statistical comparisons even as I recognized how effective they could be in winning arguments against those who were not. And I have not always been above using them myself, especially when I thought someone needed to be taken down a peg or two.

I recall a time at Marquette University when a fellow student seemed inordinately proud of his academic accomplishments at a large high school in the Twin Cities area of Minnesota and bragged about having graduated tenth in his class. Without a moment's hesitation I let him know that I was only four behind him in my high school. Remarkably, he did not ask the size of my graduating class so I did not have to tell him that it was dramatically smaller than his.

But, thanks to my youthful pancake-eating experience, I DO ask for particulars whenever I hear claims that start with "the most, the best, the largest, the safest" or any other such superlatives, which are so much a part of the language of advertising these days. And I'm very much aware that the numbers game is almost always slanted in favor the person who initiates it.

All that said, I am still occasionally troubled by my inadequacies as an eight-year-old pancake eater, no matter how much I label my experience in that department as educational.

So one day I will throw down the gauntlet (which will be made of pancake batter, of course) at my cousin's feet and challenge him to a pancake-eating contest on neutral turf.

Officials will be on hand to measure and weigh and do whatever else is necessary to assure that all "particulars" are accounted for. And I'll want a physician in attendance, just in case. Such a contest could have fatal consequences, so don't look for me to throw down that gauntlet until both Louie and I are a good deal more tired of life than we presently are. When it happens, consider yourself invited. I'll try to schedule it after the Super Bowl and before the annual Trenary Outhouse Races, when things tend to be a bit less than exciting hereabouts.

# That Was the Week That Was:
# Thank God It's Over!

ॐ

I'm writing this piece for all of my readers who have just had a bad week, because, as the old saying goes: "Misery loves company." I'll acknowledge up front that a bad week tends to be defined in the context of one's own experience, and someone out there will be inclined to say that mine was "a piece of cake" compared to his/hers. But for what it's worth, let me share it with you.

It began with a trip to Marquette General Hospital to undergo out-patient surgery to repair a hernia. I'm sorry that I don't have a more exalted anatomical location to call your attention to here, but I'm obliged to be honest, so I won't use journalistic license to convert it to a quadruple heart by-pass. I've been lucky enough to avoid a surgeon's scalpel for the past forty-four years, and what I went through, beginning this past Monday, was enough to make me want to wait another forty-four before encountering one again.

I was too naive when I had my first meeting with the surgeon to suspect anything when he told me: "You may

expect to experience some discomfort after this procedure." Knowing what I do now, I'd advise you, if you
should ever hear such a statement, to put as much distance
between yourself and its source as you can—immediately!.
Don't bother to gather up your clothing. You can explain
later to anyone in the waiting room that you happen to
know.

And be a little more suspicious of the term "out-patient"
than I was. What it means is that someone at the hospital
will knock you OUT, somebody else will cut something
OUT, and another somebody will throw you OUT—all in
one day. This division of medical responsibility lessens the
guilt that staff members would otherwise feel, knowing
what you're in for during the next several days.

The sedatives administered me before the action began
made me positively euphoric as the gurney was being
wheeled into surgery. As I was slid onto the surgical table,
I even joked to somebody that I would prefer the surgeon
limit his cutting to the side of my groin which had been
shaved. But before I could determine the impact of this
fine example of Bartol wit upon those gathered for the fes-
tivities, I was off in la-la land, and the next thing I remembered, I was back in the recovery room.

How glorious! It was all over—and I felt great! Of
course, that was because a local anesthetic had deadened
all sensations in the surgical area, and the sedative that had
sent me to la-la land hadn't yet worn off. When a nurse
helped me get upright a while later my blood pressure
dropped to 105-50, and I was very generously allowed to
hang around for another hour. But when I passed the
blood pressure test next time around, I was sent home.

What a brave and noble departure that was! I spurned
the use of a wheel chair, and on my way out I even tossed
off another witty remark to the nurse who had prepped
me for surgery. I was inordinately and foolishly proud of

myself at that moment.

Space considerations preclude my going into detail about my next five days, for which you are probably grateful. But I can tell you that I now have a greater appreciation for the simple act of sitting or lying down and getting up again. I experienced exquisite torture accomplishing those activities during that period, each move accompanied by a moan, the intensity of which was determined by Judith's proximity. When she was down in the laundry room, I skipped it entirely because it hurt too much to turn the volume up to where she could hear it.

By Thursday I was starting to feel just a bit better, but there were still three days left in the week. Not to worry! Judith went over to the home place to check on my mom, as she does every day, and came back to announce that the roof of the garage on the home place had collapsed. I had spent much of the winter removing snow from other buildings on our two properties, but never considered the garage, with its high-pitched roof, to be vulnerable to such a disaster.

To make matters worse, my son Mark's almost-classic 1985 Camaro Z28 was under all that snow, rafters, etc. For ten winters prior to this one he had stored that car in our big chicken coop, which has a roof that could support a dozen army tanks. But this year, with my father gone and garage space available, he put it in there. In my condition I can't get to the job of removing debris to see how badly damaged it is, or my Ford tractor, or the home place riding mower and all those other things one tends to store in such a structure.

It seems ironic that only three weeks ago I announced that I was reluctant to remove from the walls of that garage all those items my dad had hung there over the years. Now many of them are lying under the snow and the debris.

When I called my insurance agent, he said: "Frank, I

have some good news and some bad news for you. The good news is that there is coverage for that event in your mom's policy, but the bad news is that, though I tried, I couldn't convince your dad to increase his coverage the last time he renewed his policy, so it won't be enough."

Well, given the kind of week it's been, I'll take good news wherever I can find it—and be grateful. I'll locate someone who will be willing to buy a slightly—at least I hope it's only slightly—damaged Camaro, and I'll have a rebuilding project to keep me off the golf course this summer, where disasters for me are commonplace.

But wait a minute—it's not all over. An hour ago, when I came down to my office to write this piece, my stockinged feet began to absorb moisture from the carpeting on the floor, and I realized that the drain project I had undertaken this past fall to prevent water from seeping in during the spring snow melt hadn't worked, and the hundred dollars I had spent to reglue the carpeting after last year's water invasion would have to be spent again.

Ah, but tomorrow's Monday--a new week, a new beginning. Surely Dame Fortune wouldn't lay two bad weeks in a row on a nice guy like me——would she?

# Snow Storms: I Like Them

∾

Here in Traunik, far enough south of Lake Superior to miss the brunt of lake-effect snow and considerably north of the track that snow storms have been favoring the past several years, I sit and wait impatiently for this area to get some substantial snow amounts. Sometimes I even long for a storm that will make those of us old enough to remember it stop talking about the famous storm of '38.

I can already hear some readers saying that I should be ashamed of myself for wishing such a thing on all those people who don't share my enthusiasm for snow storms, and that I should remember how costly that storm of more than half a century ago was—and how much human suffering resulted from it. Well, I do remember, so be assured that my wishes include provisions to keep us out of harm's way.

As for suffering, we manage to inflict quite a bit upon each other in the best of weather these days, so if we're socked in by snow we can't be out on the highways—or on snowmobile trails—killing ourselves and each other. And we can't run over to our neighbor's house to settle a long-standing grudge with the weapon of our choice.

For just a short time a good old-fashioned storm can wrap a white cocoon of relative safety around us to give us a sense of security that we can't seem to find when the world is operating full tilt. My guess is that fewer deaths and injuries occur during a full-fledged snowstorm than during a so-called "normal" period.

In today's world there is such a frenzy of activity twenty-four hours a day and seven days a week that we all could profit from the brief respite a storm would provide so that we could assess whether what we've been doing makes any sense or not. What we'd learn thereby would be quite a revelation for some of us.

We'd have plenty of time to prepare for this storm, and most people wouldn't have much of an excuse for getting caught in it. Snowstorms simply can't sneak up on us the way that storm of '38 and all its predecessors did. Meteorologists begin to track them when they're still way out in the Pacific and report on their direction and speed ad infinitum and ad nauseum until the event itself is a bit anticlimactic and almost never measures up to either predictions or expectations.

Anyway, I like an occasional snow storm and that's all there is to it. And as long as I'm wishing for one, I want it to last three days. Recent ones here have been pussycats, really: twelve inches of snow, which falls for only twelve hours and is forgotten in twelve days. We need one that will get all those old-timers off the "storm of '38" kick when they talk to folks under sixty.

My mother tells me that before that one came along, she had to listen to frequent references to the storm of 1914. Right now, though, I'm willing to bet that I could stop a dozen middle-aged people on the streets of Marquette or

Escanaba before I found one who has the storm of any particular recent year on the tip of his tongue, ready for conversational action at the first mention of such phenomena. That situation has to be changed.

If there were some way to be absolutely sure that everybody could stay warm at home, or at least warm enough not to be in danger, I'd ask for a power failure during the storm, too. It would be good for us to eat cold beans for supper, sopping up the juice with a piece of untoasted bread to clean the dish off, and then having a little dry cereal and milk out of the same dish the next morning for breakfast. Going without all those things that are operated by electricity in our homes for a while would remind us how much easier we have it (I said "easier," not "better") than our grandparents did.

Without television to distract us, we might even have meaningful conversations with other family members. Maybe we'd play a game of Scrabble, Chinese checkers, or euchre by candlelight. And we wouldn't be tempted to watch Oprah Winfrey truck out some folks who, as kids, hid under the bed when their parents made love and became dysfunctional adults as a result. Tell me now, would a good old-fashioned whizz bang of a storm be such a terrible idea?

# Damn the Buffet! Take It Away!

∾

S tatistics about the number of overweight people in the United States have been getting more and more attention in the media lately. And well they should, because they are frightening. Criteria to determine whom to include in the category "overweight" vary, but even those that are the kindest to the chubbies among us place more than a third of us in the group.

The seven-day automobile trip I took to North Carolina three weeks ago brought dramatically to my attention one of the causes of this phenomenon: those increasingly popular breakfast buffets in the chain restaurants most of us patronize when we're on the road. Buffets of any kind are culprits, because they all encourage diners to "pig out." But breakfast buffets are especially nasty because of the number of fat-laden items they offer.

It took us a long time to get around to labeling cigarettes and alcoholic beverages as hazardous to our health, and we'll probably never get around to doing the same with breakfast buffets. But we should. There ought to be a huge sign over every one proclaiming: "Warning! What you are likely to select from the items available here may lead to your premature death."

I've felt this way for quite a while, but on this trip, during which we ate breakfast on the road five times, three of those times in restaurants with breakfast buffets, I observed what folks were piling onto their dishes from them. A few conclusions from my observations follow:

(1) Those diners whose bulk suggested that over-eating was a chronic problem for them were the most likely to choose the buffet over items from the regular menu, and their plates were filled to overflowing with high-fat foods like bacon and pork sausage.

(2) Eggs, French toast, bacon, and pork sausage tended to be much in evidence on the plates of ALL buffet visitors, and in amounts that I estimated far exceeded maximum daily recommendations for fat and salt intake. I suspect what motivated those choices was, at least in part, the notion that one should try to get more for his money by loading up on expensive items.

(3) Even though the contents of some of those buffet tables made it possible for a diner to select a "heart smart" breakfast of dry cereal, fruit, toast, etc., almost nobody did.

I confess that my personal reason for avoiding such buffets is that I have a whole lot more will power than won't power, and on those rare occasions when I go the buffet route I walk away from it with a calorie-, fat-, and salt-laden plateful of food. Let's face it, it would take a person with considerably more discipline than yours truly and most people reading this essay to walk past all those deep-fried goodies whose aroma practically shouts: "Take me," and head, instead, for the melon slices, bran flakes, skim milk, etc.—when those are available. What do I order for breakfast on the road?—-two fried eggs over medium, two sausage patties—fried crisp, hash browns (or American fries), whole wheat toast, and, of course, coffee—please, not decaffeinated. Quite a calorie and fat load there, too, but a finite one. Two sausage patties can't hurt me as much as six, and two fried eggs are nothing compared to those huge piles of scrambled ones I watched folks lug to their tables.

And that's my point: breakfast and other buffets almost force us to over-eat. I'm being totally serious when I say that they really ought to be outlawed. Now that cigarettes are finally being subjected to some regulation, no single act by our government would go farther to protect our nation's health than such a ban, especially now that more meals are being eaten in restaurants than at home.

I have one other quarrel with buffets: they represent just one more disconnect between people. On my way to North Carolina I bought gasoline at a self-serve station, stuck my credit card into a slot to pay for it, and then watched my receipt pop out of another slot. On one of the tollways I threw coins into a machine so that a red light would turn green and I could go on my way.

I am almost certain that a decade from now, restaurants will be as automated as gas stations already are. Diners will shove a card into a slot, wait for a receipt to appear, go down a line for food dispensed by robots to fill stomachs that will be even larger than most are today, and then shove their receipts into another slot to activate a turnstile which will spew them back into the parking lot—all this without seeing any other human beings except fellow diners.

So while it is still an option for me, when I go to a restaurant I head for a booth or table and wait to be served. And I cringe only a little when an occasional waitress asks: "What would youse like?" How much friendlier those four words are than the computerized ones which will soon replace them. As for the obligatory query: "How is everything?" I don't even mind that, because I know that at least once in a while the asker really cares.

Mostly, though, I'll avoid those buffets whenever possible because, at the same time that they are elevating profits for restaurant owners, they are doing the same for my cholesterol, blood pressure, calorie count, etc. and I can do a pretty good job of that without their help, thank you.

# Birdfeeders, Dogs, and Houseplants Can Ruin a Vacation

∾

As a columnist I feel obliged to at least occasionally offer my readers some useful information. Be advised that this is one of those times, and be further advised that you move your eyes away from the following paragraphs without reading them at your own peril—particularly if you are a married man, are within a decade or so of retirement, and would like to do a bit of winter traveling when you get there.

"Birdfeeders, dogs, and houseplants"—-repeat those words at least half a dozen times and follow each repetition with "No, no, no! That will set the stage for proper attention to what I'm about to share with you, which will in turn greatly increase the likelihood that when cabin fever threatens to overwhelm you during some post-retirement winter, you'll be able to sojourn for a few weeks in a climate a bit warmer than the one you deal with in the U.P. from December through March. The first houseplant to invade our home in Traunik, shortly after we moved into it thirty-seven years ago, was a variegated philodendron—

-and it hasn't left yet! The heartiest of plants, it thrived no matter what Judith did or didn't do to it, which inspired her to bring in others that would offer her more of a horticultural challenge. She has certainly accomplished that with the twenty-seven (but who's counting) that can now be found in every room in our house—tastefully placed, I must add, because Judith is a woman of good taste.

I am looking at two right now that are doing penance in my basement office, relegated here by their failure to behave themselves properly in choicer locations upstairs. I think they've gotten the message, though, because both have decided to bloom and do other things to curry my favor in the wake of friend wife's announcement that she doesn't see how we can take that three-week trip "somewhere south" that I've been starting to promote, because those plants need tender loving care at least once a week.

And tender loving care is what they get from her. She moves from one to the other, a misting bottle in one hand, a damp cloth in the other, and a sprinkling can clamped between her teeth, dispensing exactly the right treatment to each. She's not likely to entrust their care to anyone with less expertise in the area than Martha Stewart, whom, if I get desperate enough, I will try to employ.

I don't know how Martha is with birds and dogs. Just yesterday, as Judith and I were looking out our window at purple finches, grosbeaks, goldfinches, nuthatches, and assorted other creatures of the avian world feeding frenziedly but happily at our birdfeeder, she asked me if I was willing to condemn those lovely creatures to almost certain death by not being around to fill that feeder for three weeks. She announced that she had just read somewhere that once birds get used to a daily diet of black oil sunflower seeds they are rendered incapable of utilizing tree buds etc.

She dispenses such wisdom sparingly, and only to make a point—the point this time being, if you haven't yet figured it out, that she really doesn't want to go anywhere for three weeks in the winter, thank you, and is quite content with life if she can only get to the library for her weekly quota of ten books, which she spends much of her time reading when she is not misting and sprinkling.

Just this morning she opened the door that leads into our entryway, where Jake, our German shepherd was taking his morning ease, and asked me if I'd look into his eyes. Being a dutiful and obedient husband and thinking that Jake might be suffering from some kind of ocular distress which I would be expected to take care of, I did as she asked. At which point she said: "Can you look straight into that dog's eyes and tell him that you're prepared to abandon him for three long weeks. You know how lonesome he gets when we're gone just for the day."

It is a relentless campaign she is waging, and I fear that she is winning it. So before she fires the next salvo, I may as well make the best deal that I can with her. I think I can get her to agree not to spray me with the misting bottle whenever she's about her horticultural husbandry. She says she does it so that I can know how good the plants feel, but I really don't enjoy it all that much.

And I'll try to get her to play a game of Scrabble anytime I request it during the month of February (which is when I wanted to take that trip). What the heck: why not go for broke! For the rest of the winter not one more reference to my "slovenly habit" (her words) of throwing the newspaper on the floor when I'm finished with it. We'll do the South when the dog dies, the plants wilt, and Holmquist's Feed Mill in Trenary stops selling black oil sunflower seeds.

But if only someone had told me about "birdfeeders, dogs, and houseplants NO! NO! NO!" ten years ago, I'd be writing this essay from some Caribbean island, and on a far different subject.

# Snowbirds: I Still Don't Want to Be One

ॐ

Several years ago I wrote the following words about those folks who "escape" the Upper Peninsula each winter in favor of such warm-weather places as Florida and Arizona:

"I will never understand snowbirds. They have tolerated the sequential onslaught of mosquito, black fly, noseeum, deer fly, and wasp; endured the weekly summer chore of mowing lawns that refused to look neat for more than a day at a time; pretended to enjoy the visits of hundreds of relatives from the city all summer; and, when autumn came, raked up leaves and other summer residue from their yards.

"Then just at the point when all that kind of activity was behind them and they could look forward to an insect-free, chore-free (except for occasional snow shoveling), and relative-free period of peace and quiet, they have insisted upon loading their automobiles with insect spray, golf clubs, sun-tan lotion, summer clothes, and other paraphernalia of summer and driven a couple of thousand miles to do more of the same in Florida, Arizona, or some other warm-weather winter spot.

"Someday social scientists will look back upon this irrational behavior of thousands of citizens of America's northern states as an unexplainable blip on the screen of man's progress toward common sense. There'll be no other way to deal with their voluntary rejection of the most beautiful season of the year up here: winter."

For the record, I haven't changed my mind about that, but the lake effect snow machine certainly has been doing its utmost to get me to do so this winter. Were I writing about snowbirds today, I would definitely not use the phrase "except for occasional snow shoveling" because there has not been a day in the past week when I haven't had to engage in that activity. I just climbed down from the roof of my workshop after spending several hours there removing thirty-eight inches of snow (a tape measure total, not a guess) from it. A collapsed barn roof just a mile down the road had reminded me it was time to do that chore.

And this past weekend county plows and Mother Nature combined to pile snow so high at the end of the driveway that my snow thrower, the largest walk-behind available, could make almost no progress against it. I know now that the winter of 1996-97 is likely to be a record breaker for snowfall, a possibility substantiated by a National Weather Service report that in my area we're thirty inches ahead of last year at this time—-and the winter of 1995-96 was itself a record breaker!

Mountains of snow notwithstanding, I remain an ardent fan of winter and cannot imagine being out of the U.P. during it except for maybe a three-week sojourn away from the snow to ward off late-season cabin fever. For me winter scenery, especially the kind we're treated to when a heavy snowfall is followed by a couple of bright, sunny days, even surpasses in beauty any that we can encounter during the other season of beauty—autumn.

I enjoy snowshoeing through the cedar swamps and hardwood forests near our house, even when my dog Jake steps on the tail of one of my snowshoes and sends me headlong into a drift, or a cedar bough unloads its burden of white stuff down my back, or a binding snaps and I have to improvise one from my boot laces. There's no frustration on my snowshoe trails to compare with that suffered by those snowbirds on southern golf courses, who contend with traffic jams on their way to the course and even worse ones on the course itself. And at the end of MY sporting activity, Judith never asks me what my score was!

Mostly, though, I like staying put for the winter because doing so keeps me connected with my community in a way that no snowbird can be. I'm not prepared to abandon my role as a member of the community, attending social functions, occasionally offering my services to organizations that need them, cheering my basketball team on and complimenting one of its players whom I encounter in a local business place—in short, being part of the mix that helps a town, or for that matter a rural area, thrive.

Snowbirds play a lot of golf, shuffleboard, and bridge. They drink afternoon cocktails, during which they discuss which local restaurant has the best "early bird" deals. But they are attached in no meaningful way to the community they are residing in for the winter.

I know whereof I speak because I have quite a few snowbird friends, who will probably remain my friends after they've read this essay because they'll assume that winter cold has frozen my brain and rendered me incapable of exercising the good judgment they have.

Will I ever change my views on this subject? Perhaps, when the debility that often comes with aging forces me to the sidelines of life. But I will never delude myself into thinking that I'm in the mainstream when I get there—and I don't think I'll like it very much.

# Santa Claus Still Is Coming to Town—
# I Think!

∾

Ithink it was Voltaire who said: "If there were no God then it would be necessary to invent Him." He was speaking, of course, of man's need for the spiritual in his life. On a considerably less lofty level he might also have said that even though there is no Santa Claus (or whatever his counterpart would be called in France), he has been a necessary invention for folks who spend several of their growing-up years believing in him.

I say this because the inevitable disconnect with a belief in Santa that occurs in most of us at about the age of six or seven prepares us for a whole series of abandonments of childhood notions on our way to an adult belief system.

I don't remember precisely, or for that matter even vaguely, when hard physical evidence against literal acceptance of Santa Claus and his eight reindeer gave me my first significant nudge toward the adulthood that awaited me a decade or so down the line, but I recall with painful clarity an event that generated my first feelings of skepticism—-skepticism heavily mixed with a sense of guilt at my impending apostasy.

Today's kids see a Santa Claus on every corner and in every shopping mall and therefore probably realize early on that there is some fakery going on with the whole business. But my Santa existed only in my imagination, put there by "The Night Before Christmas" and other such yuletide stories, so believing in him came easy for me.

Thus, when I rummaged around the nooks and crannies of the then unfinished upstairs of our home one snowy December day and found in one of them the gifts that my mother and dad had hidden there to await their placement under the tree on Christmas morning, I was both dumbfounded and excited.

In those "mom stays home and dad goes to work" days before World War II, kids usually wound up reporting such earth-shaking finds to their mothers. Which is what I did as fast as my stubby little legs could navigate the steep steps back down to the kitchen, where my mother was preparing supper. I suppose she was a bit disappointed at her failure to do a better job of hiding those gifts that were to come from Santa. But the only emotion she displayed to me was sympathy because I had discovered "Santa's hiding place" (not my parents') and, as she told me in what I now know was a mock serious tone, the jolly fat man in the red suit had been known to become decidedly unjolly when that happened.

I had no doubt about his knows-all-sees-all ability, having had it pounded into my head often by the lyrics of "Santa Claus Is Coming to Town," so I bought the likelihood of his displeasure with me hook, line, and sinker, a displeasure that, according to my mother, usually took the form of his removing those gifts from his no-longer-secret hiding place and giving them to a little boy who had not been as snoopy as I.

But good mothers—and my mother was, and is, one of

the best—always leave hope with their children, whatever else they might have to take away from them as they steer them toward adulthood. So mine said that Santa might relent and not take such a drastic course of action if he received nothing but glowing reports about my behavior from that day until Christmas (clever lady, she!).

I have no memory of just what I did specifically during the eternity between then and Christmas to assure such reports, but I'm quite sure that I brought goodness to a new level that no Santa Claus spy could fail to notice.

Above all, I resisted all impulses to climb those stairs again to see if those gifts had been plucked away by one of Santa's helpers, because that way I was sure lay disaster. And though, even then, I was inclined to talk more than I should, I obeyed my mother's instructions and said not a word about my discovery to my brother or my two sisters.

When Christmas morning finally came, every one of those items that I had spotted in the upstairs hiding place was under the tree, so I knew that my recent good behavior had gained me a reprieve. But my relief at learning I had not gone giftless also released me to look at that whole chain of events from another angle, one that planted seeds of skepticism which would germinate into serious doubt before the next Christmas rolled around and full-blown disbelief by the one after that.

But now, six decades later, I still believe in the idea of Santa Claus and have several times donned a Santa suit and ho-hoed my way into the headstart classroom just down the road from our house during the Christmas program there. The earnestness with which many youngsters told me what was on their Christmas wish list and the flippancy with which others tried to pull my beard off as they sat on my lap suggested that the Santa myth, though still alive and well, is not as universally accepted by four-year-

olds as it once was.

That's okay. We all take our myths where we find them and, as I said at the outset of this piece, we lay them aside throughout our lives as we find they no longer serve us. But while they do serve us our lives are enriched by them—and that is all the argument we should need to keep the Santa Claus myth alive.

# Baby Pictures and New Year's: A Connection

∾

I t's over for another year! The untrimming of the Christmas tree and its removal have been accomplished; the greeting cards we received this year have been tied into a bundle to season for a year before being tossed out to make room for the next batch; and all the Christmas goodies baked at our place or sent to us have been dutifully consumed, with yours truly performing most of that particular duty—and loving every moment of it!

Only our memories of Christmas, 1996, remain—and four delightful snapshots of very young children, all under two years old, sent us by their proud parents along with their cards. They're posted on our refrigerator door now, and there they will stay far into the new year to remind us that life begins in confidence and hope, which it is our responsibility as adults to nourish and support, not destroy.

Nicholas, the oldest, dressed like the big boy he will all too soon become, sits in front of a Christmas tree, head cocked slightly, only a trace of a smile on his handsome face, which signals that he's ready for whatever's out there, and he expects it to be good.

Dondo, who received his nickname (for "Don") almost as soon as he was born, has the most puckish look of the four. Dressed in tan bib overalls decorated with cartoon animal characters, he's sitting back in a very relaxed pose. His feet, stretched forward and thus considerably closer to the camera than the rest of him, look larger than they really are, but in doing so convey the message that he'll shortly be using them to get into the friendly mischief that his expression promises. Blake Edward is wearing a smile wide enough and sincere enough to melt the heart of the most dedicated Christmas Scrooge around. He's also wearing a Green Bay Packers sweat shirt, sitting quite erect in it, and holding his hands together as if cradling a football. I doubt that even the most rabid Detroit Lions fan could resist shifting his allegiance, at least for a moment, upon encountering that snapshot.

Finally there is Katrina Ann, my only blood relative in the group, the rest being related to me through friendship. She's also the youngest and, as her name indicates, the only girl. She's wearing a garment appropriate to her age, a white sleeper, which highlights a pretty face framed in dark hair so abundant that it must have started growing when she was no more than a gleam in her father's eye. Her smile is the most delicate, the most vulnerable of the four, and it is directed at her mother, off-camera except for hands ready to protect Katrina and embrace her again after the picture-taking session.

I'm not very likely to be around when these four promising youngsters reach adulthood, but that's okay, because their parents are. And because all four of these "first" children were born to folks who wanted them badly and who are temperamentally well equipped to do the nurturing and nudging necessary to get them to adulthood, I like their chances at this point.

But the prospect of their wearing the same smiles in adulthood as those so delightfully in evidence in the pictures just described will depend upon much more than the loving care of parents. So I find myself, on this first day of a new year, hoping that the world of 2015 will be different in several important ways from the one I can look back on.

I hope that Blake Edward, Dondo, Nicholas, and Katrina will become adults in a world not so enamored of money as ours seems to be; that, without destroying our free enterprise system, we will somehow have been able by then to achieve a better financial balance in this country than the one which now has almost fifty percent of its wealth concentrated in the top one percent of its population.

I hope, also, that when my "refrigerator four" grow up they won't feel the need to have handguns and other weapons within arm's reach in order to achieve personal safety, which is a solution to the violence problem in this country that, in my judgment, is being recommended by too many of the folks in MY generation.

I further hope that eighteen years from now it will be more fashionable to be an environmentalist than it presently is; that seeing our earth as a very small ship on a very large ocean—a ship that needs tender loving care—will represent conventional wisdom rather than a "fringe" point of view.

Finally, I hope that by 2015 we will truly become the melting pot that we've always bragged about being, and that my grandchildren will be able to marry into black, brown, or yellow families without the raising of a single eyebrow anywhere along a color continuum that will be so blurred as to make everyone truly socially color blind.

When I expressed these hopes to a good friend the other night as we sat at a corner table in the Log Cabin

Restaurant eating breast of chicken smothered in raspberry sauce (wonderful!), drinking fine wine, and in general enjoying the lifestyle it has been our good fortune to attain, he told me I was living in a fool's paradise if I really believed any of those hopes could be attained, and he gave me some strange looks for even thinking they ought to be.

I hope his views aren't yours, and if they are, you'll tolerate mine during these final days of this season of good cheer. May the upcoming year be good to you and to all the those kids whose pictures are posted on YOUR refrigerator door.

# A New Year's Resolution—for Judith

❧

I wish Judith were inclined to make New Year's resolutions, because I have one in mind for her which might not improve her life too much but would have a salutary effect on mine. Here is how it would read: "I resolve not to utter the five words 'and while you're at it' in the direction of my beloved husband even once this year."

She did it again this morning as I sat in my recliner looking out at a horde of goldfinches, chickadees, and grosbeaks fluttering around an empty birdfeeder and announced my intention to fill it as soon as I finished a post-breakfast cup of coffee, which has become a ritual for me in recent years.

On the face of it such a statement would not seem to have much potential to generate those dreaded five words, but Judith is nothing if not resourceful in such matters, and her eyes, in scanning the locale of the proposed action, zeroed in immediately on a pile of something that had been deposited there by Flash, a basset hound who was our houseguest for Christmas along with our son and daughter-in-law.

Apparently our resident German shepherd was so entranced by this strange-looking canine specimen he was frolicking with that he forgot to tell her that a deposit of that sort on our deck just a few feet from the largest window in our house was a very strong no-no. So I forgave Flash immediately but was less inclined to extend that forgiveness to Judith, who ought to have seen that steam was still rising from the pile she said I ought to remove "while I was at it."

The contrast between the chore she had in mind for me and the one I had thought of myself was pretty dramatic. There is something kind of noble about going out into the cold and snow with a scoop full of bird seed, just as there is something decidedly ignoble about going out there with a "pooper scooper."

I'm proud to say I drew the line at that one, and birds feeding on the sunflower seed have begun to drop husks on the evidence, which I expect snow predicted for tonight to completely obliterate—at least until spring.

Why is it that wives always assume that if their husbands are at one thing they might just as well be doing something else at the same time? And why is it that so often the "something else" takes much more time and energy than the original task? Once when I prepared to take out the garbage, Judith suggested that I wash the car and the pickup, and as long as both vehicles were outside, sweep the garage floor "while I was at it." If she had not been slightly off her best form that day she would have thrown in remodeling the porch in the guesthouse without breaking a sweat.

To her credit she usually appends these requests to activities that I am preparing to do or am already engaged in. But she defines the latter somewhat loosely. She is capable, on one of her better days, to say: "As long as you just exhaled why don't you get the mail—and while you're at it, drive over to the Limestone Mini-Mall for a gallon of milk."

I am least inclined to be annoyed by her while-you're-at-it-itis when I say that I am driving to Marquette to take care of this or that business. Not that she doesn't perform admirably in that situation. In fact, her requests are impressive enough to require listing—numbered in the order which they are to be performed (she is a paragon of organization).

I've been known to get so caught up in following those numbered instructions that I never get around to my own errands. But I don't mind, because these are highly visible activities (I want the world to know when I'm at work), and they give me an opportunity to interact with my fellow man in a way that the chore with which I started this piece certainly does not.

On the outside chance that this will be the year for a Judith New Year's resolution, I'll drop a hint to her about it. Now would be a good time. She just volunteered to cut me some fruit cake and potica to snack on while I watch the football game, and I suggested that while she's at it she might consider brewing me a cup of coffee, too.